Conflict Resolution and the Structure of the State System

AN ANALYSIS OF ARBITRATIVE SETTLEMENTS

Conflict Resolution and the Structure of the State System

AN ANALYSIS OF ARBITRATIVE SETTLEMENTS

Gregory A. Raymond

ALLANHELD OSMUN, Publishers
SIJTHOFF & NOORDHOFF International Publishers

Published in the United States of America in 1980
by Allanheld, Osmun & Co. Publishers, Inc.
19 Brunswick Road, Montclair, New Jersey 07042

Published in The Netherlands in 1980
by Sijthoff & Noordhoff International Publishers bv
Alphen aan den Rijn/ The Netherlands
ISBN 90 286 0319 0

LIBRARY OF CONGRESS CATALOGING IN PUBLICATION DATA

Raymond, Gregory A
   Conflict resolution and the structure of the state
system.

   Includes index.
   1. Arbitration, International.   2.   International
relations.   I.   Title.
JX1952.R334   341.5'2   79-53702
ISBN 0-916672-12-3

Printed in the United States of America

Contents

Tables and Figures

Figures

Preface

One of the most notable trends in the academic study of international relations has been the recent resurgence of interest in international law. Students of global jurisprudence have again begun to integrate their analyses of international norms with an examination of the political atmosphere in which law-making occurs, and many have suggested that various dimensions of the international legal order can be measured. If this is so, then one could argue that it is possible to test theories about the ties between international law and interstate behavior. Moreover, various signs indicate that this emphasis upon empirical theorizing is becoming increasingly prevalent. Distinguished scholars such as Richard A. Falk, Wesley L. Gould, and Michael Barkun have urged researchers to go beyond impressionism and adopt the methods of social science. Two past presidents of the American Society of International Law (Oscar Schachter and Brunson MacChesney) have also called for the use of these methods in theory-building, and the Society's Board of Reviews and Development has sponsored several activities in an attempt to carry out their recommendations. As a consequence of this rising momentum, the field of international law presently is experiencing a methodological revolution similar to those which have previously influenced the conduct of research in virtually all the other cognate behavioral sciences.

This study is an outgrowth of my interest in applying quantitative methods to the study of legal phenomena. During the past five years, at several professional conferences, I have attempted to use these methods to analyze various modes of conflict resolution. Since arbitration has been employed to resolve international disputes in many different cultural settings throughout recorded history, I felt that it warranted more attention from social scientists than it seemed to have received. In particular, it appeared to me that a reconnaissance study was needed to obtain a general picture of the possible causes and consequences of arbitral activity. Hence the central aims of this book are to determine empirically: (1) the extent to which specific cultural and structural attributes of international system are associated with the use of arbitration; and (2) the impact of arbitration upon the onset of war.

I realize that I have incurred numerous intellectual debts during the preparation of this study. One can never repay these debts but can acknowledge the many individuals who contributed their ideas, thoughtful criticisms, and support.

I am especially indebted to Charles W. Kegley, Jr. Under his tutelage I have benefited more than he will ever know.

My sincere appreciation must also be expressed to James A. Kuhlman for his interest in my work and his generous support for my research efforts.

A number of scholars provided insightful commentaries on different portions of the original draft of this book. Because of their observations, I was forced to clarify and refine much of my initial thinking. The list of these individuals is too long to be included in its entirety; however, Robert M. Rood and George D. Haimbaugh deserve special mention.

I would also like to thank Willard M. Overgaard for his constant support and encouragement, and Pat Durie for her frequent clerical assistance. I am especially grateful to Carol Dahlberg for typing the bulk of the manuscript with both speed and skill. The editorial board at Allanheld, Osmun &

Company also deserves a note of thanks for putting up with my miscalculated deadlines.

My deepest gratitude, however, goes to my wife, Christine, whose patience and unwaivering faith in my ability helped in more ways than can be measured. Finally, I would like to indicate my overall indebtedness to the members of my family, using, I must add, the most inclusive meaning of that term. It is only proper that this book be dedicated to them.

G. A. R.

Boise, Idaho
March 1979

Too many people assume, generally without having given any serious thought to its character or its history, that international law is and always has been a sham. Others seem to think that it is a force without inherent strength of its own, and that if only we had the sense to set the lawyers to work to draft a comprehensive code for the nations, we might live together in peace and all would be well with the world. Whether the cynic or the sciolist is the less helpful is hard to say, but both of them make the same mistake. They both assume that international law is a subject on which anyone can form his opinions intuitively, without taking the trouble, as one has to do with other subjects, to inquire into the relevant facts.

—J. L. Brierly

Introduction

According to legend, Poseidon and Helios once quarreled over the possession of Corinthian territory. In order to settle the dispute peacefully, the hundred-handed giant, Briareus, listened to the rival claims of each party and subsequently awarded the isthmus to the sea god and the surrounding highlands to the god of the sun.[1] Underlying this myth is a theme about conflict resolution procedures which is woven throughout the fabric of Occidental thought: the efficacy of third-party arbitration as an amicable means of settling disputes.

   Though cases involving the use of arbitration can be found in Mesopotamia during the third millennium B.C., its practice first became widespread in the seventh century B.C. when it spread from the Greek city-states on the Balkan Peninsula to their colonies scattered through islands in the Aegean and Ionian seas. These arbitrations focused primarily on establishing a general framework for the political reconciliation of disputants, and only secondarily upon achieving a technically satisfactory liquidation of the immediate issue.[2] The arbitrations were carried out among the members of a given league and, to a lesser extent, between opposing confederations. In each instance arbiters usually were selected from the citizenry of a neutral *polis*, but at times, groups of city-states, league assemblies, and the Delphic oracle functioned as *amiable compositeurs*. By the time of the Hellenistic Age, arbitration had become a commonly adopted mode of pacific redress. Treaties often included compromisory clauses binding the contracting parties to arbitrate future differences, and states such as Rhodes gained wide recognition for their arbitrative skills.

With the ascendancy of Rome, this long standing approach to arbitration began to change. Although some arbitrations during the *pax romana* did occur between Rome and other powers, in the main they centered upon controversies among states inside Rome's imperial orbit. Thus, rather than arbitration functioning as a conflict resolution procedure between independent states, it became a method by which the Senate (or its appointees) could adjudicate differences within a large and heterogeneous empire. Arbitration, in short, began to assume the character of litigation. Whereas ancient Greek arbitrations pertained to the interstate political relationships which surrounded a dispute, Roman jurisprudence engendered a trend toward dealing with the legal technicalities of the dispute itself.

Interstate arbitrations in medieval Europe initially were very similar due to the political primacy of the arbitrator. Claimants, instead of being subordinated to the secular power of Rome, were subject to the sacral authority of the papacy.[3] But once ecclesiastical influence over diplomatic matters declined, arbitral awards increasingly were decided by peers on the basis of equity rather than by virtue of the third party's claim to universal supremacy. Throughout the high Middle Ages, arbitrations of this sort transpired between the Italian city-states, and, by the fifteenth century, they took place among the Swiss cantons and the towns comprising the Hanseatic League. Nevertheless, the use of arbitration continued to be "irregular and spasmodic" until the 1794 Jay Treaty between Great Britain and the United States, since which time its practice has assumed a certain "regularity and system."[4]

Given the existence of a patterned regularity in arbitrations during the nineteenth and twentieth centuries, it should be possible to generalize about the causes and consequences of arbitral activity. The specific goals of this book are to determine empirically: (1) the extent to which certain systemic conditions have been associated with the use of arbitration as a mode of conflict resolution, and (2) the impact international arbitration has had upon the onset of war. The rationale for these goals is quite simple. On the one hand, arbitration historically has been considered a powerful tool for settling disputes, and, on the other, war has long been seen as one of the most serious problems facing the international community. Despite these facts, very little data-based research has been done on either the conditions which give rise to arbitration or its effectiveness in reducing the incidence of war.

The failure to examine these kinds of issues may be attributed to several factors. In the first place, students of international law often deny that the scientific method can be used in their work.

Rather, they write as lawyers to win would-be cases for their self-chosen clients, as prosecutors to indict self-chosen defendents, as self-appointed legislators to create or revise new international legal norms, as self-appointed judges to clarify and apply existing international norms and, finally, as self-appointed legal advisors to inform their government as to the legal implications of its actions.[5]

In the second place, "Law as a science is widely distrusted or scorned, sometimes feared by representatives of other scientific disciplines as some kind of secular priesthood."[6] Thus, although the legal-analytic research technique contributed to the intellectual foundation of the field of international relations, and scholars such as Gentilli, Pierino Belli, and Balthasar de Ayala were catalysts in secularizing international relations theory, many contemporary scientists have neglected the field of international law in general, and topics such as arbitration in particular.

The central theme of this study is that the current gulf separating legal and scientific scholarship is neither necessary nor constructive. Legal norms contain both factual and valuational components. When approached from the former perspective, they may be analyzed scientifically, since the investigator seeks only to establish their existence and ascertain their impact, not to appraise their transcendental validity. As Barkun has put it, "Law is not simply another discipline to be borrowed when lacunae in one's vocabulary so demand. . . . It must, for social scientists, be a datum before it is a professional orientation, a field of humanistic study, or a set of institutions in one's immediate environment."[7]

Needless to say, if data can be derived from the information contained in the amorphous mass of international law which has accumulated during centuries of jurisprudence, then many previously neglected research questions would become amenable to quantitative analysis. But where should one begin? A recent survey of the field of international law which was sympathetic to the aims of quantitative analysis asserted that "much work needs to be done on changes in the law that take place concurrently with or as a consequence of basic changes in the international system."[8] Similarly, another survey noted that a quantitative analysis of international law could prove useful "if trends in the law were measured and these trends correlated with other forms of social change."[9] As a result of these suggestions, plus Hoffmann's contention that research should begin "by stressing the links between international law and historical international systems,"[10] this study will begin by examining the impact temporal changes in various properties of the international system have had upon the use of arbitration.

The figure below outlines the analytic approach that will guide the analysis which follows. It assumes that changes in the amount of arbitral activity within the international system may be accounted for by the additive impact of changes in the system's cultural and structural attributes. The cultural attributes that will be examined fall into two distinct clusters: legal norms which pertain to the use of force (e.g., beliefs about the importance of military necessity, just war, neutrality, etc.), and legal norms which pertain to pacific modes of dispute settlement (e.g., beliefs about the importance of arbitration, mediation, conciliation, etc.). By way of contrast, the structural attributes make up three clusters: (1) capability distribution (i.e., the degree of concentration and movement); (2) status hierarchy (i.e., the degree of inconsistency and mobility); and (3) intergovernmental bonds (i.e., the amount of alliance aggregation and international organization formation). Throughout this study, theoretical literature bearing upon the variables within these clusters will be examined to find propositions which relate changes in specific systemic attributes to changes in the amount of arbitral activity. Whenever such propositions are found, they will be transformed into testable hypotheses and subjected to empirical analysis.

A Schematic Outline of the Research Foci under Investigation

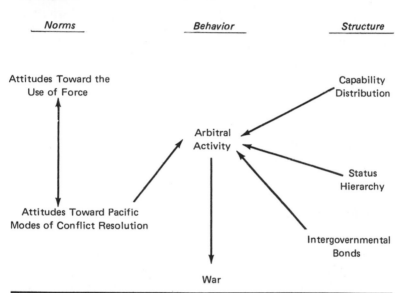

Each of the ensuing chapters in this volume can be viewed schematically as a sequential step in the process of testing those propositions which pertain to the goals discussed earlier. Chapter 1 defines the concept of arbitration in operational terms. Chapter 2 focuses on the relationship between attitudes toward force and attitudes toward pacific methods of dispute settlement. In addition, it examines the impact of the latter on the amount of arbitral activity that occurs within the international system. Chapter 3 analyzes the extent to which capability distribution, status hierarchy, and intergovernmental bonds affect arbitration. Chapter 4 uses the results from the two previous chapters in a comparison of the relative potency of cultural and structural attributes when explaining historical changes in the amount of international arbitration. Finally, Chapter 5 moves away from those systemic conditions which have been associated with the use of arbitration and goes on to probe the impact that arbitration has had upon the outbreak of war. In sum, this study has been organized to progress from a univariate analysis of first-order propositions about arbitration, to a bivariate analysis of second-order propositions, and ultimately to a multivariate analysis of the linkages between these propositions. The first step in this process involves conceptualizing arbitration in a manner that lends itself to observation and measurement. Hence, let us now turn to the problem of operationalizing the concept of arbitral activity.

Notes

1. Jackson H. Ralston, *International Arbitration from Athens to Locarno* (Stanford, Cal.: Stanford University Press, 1929), p. 153.

2. Adda B. Bozeman, *Politics and Culture in International History* (Princeton: Princeton University Press, 1960), p. 83. See also Coleman Phillipson, *International Law and Custom of Ancient Greece and Rome,* 2 vols. (London: Macmillan & Co., 1911); and Marcus N. Todd, *International Arbitration Amongst the Greeks* (Oxford: Clarendon Press, 1963).

3. A parallel may be seen in the Islamic world. The Prophet Muhammad not only respected the traditional Arabic practice of arbitration, but he often acted as an arbitrator himself. Majid Khadduri, "An Introduction to the Islamic Law of Nations," in *Comparative World Politics, Readings in Western and Premodern Non-Western International Relations,* ed. Joel Larus (Belmont, Cal.: Wadsworth Publishing Company, 1964), p. 237.

4. Ralston, *International Arbitration,* p. 191. The Jay Treaty provided for the arbitration of three disputes between the United Kingdom and the United States: (1) the boundary of the St. Croix River, (2) the recovery of debts owed to British merchants by citizens of the United States, and (3) ascertaining the losses and damages suffered by U.S. citizens as a result of British maritime seizures.

5. William D. Coplin, "Current Studies of the Functions of International Law," in *Political Science Annual: An International Review,* ed. James A. Robinson, II (Indianapolis, Ind.: Bobbs-Merrill Company, 1970), pp. 160–61.

6. Vilhelm Aubert, "Courts and Conflict Resolution," *Journal of Conflict Resolution* 11 (March 1961): 50. As Hoffmann points out, this

attitude is not restricted to the natural sciences: "Social scientists are impatient with a discipline that seems to focus exclusively either on a closed universe of norms—their logical consequences, their hierarchy, their interconnections—divorced from the political and social universe in which they appear and which they try to regulate, or on doctrinal interpretations and desiderata that, while they take political and social purposes into account, represent only the idiosyncratic views of irrelevant if respected writers." Stanley Hoffmann, *The State of War* (New York: Frederick A. Praeger, 1965), pp. 123–24.

7. Michael Barkun, *Law Without Sanction: Order in Primitive Societies and the World Community* (New Haven: Yale University Press, 1968), p. 11.

8. Wesley L. Gould and Michael Barkun, *International Law and the Social Sciences* (Princeton: Princeton University Press, 1970), p. 209.

9. Nicholas G. Onuf, "International Law-in-Action and the Numbers Game: A Comment," *International Studies Quarterly* 14 (September 1970): 333.

10. Stanley Hoffmann, "The Study of International Law and the Theory of International Relations," *Proceedings of the Fifty-Seventh Annual Meeting of the American Society of International Law* (Washington, D.C., 1963), p. 30.

CHAPTER 1

The Quest for an Empirical Theory of International Arbitration

It is impossible to attack as a transgressor he who offers to lay his grievances before a tribunal of arbitration.
                                        —Archidamus

The Concept of Arbitration

The first recorded case of international arbitration occurred during the third millenium B.C. in Mesopotamia. Lagash, Umma, and Kish were three of about fifteen politically autonomous but economically interdependent Sumerian city-states. When Lagash and Umma clashed over a boundary question, the king of Kish settled their dispute in accordance with an award that allegedly had been revealed to him by the God Enlil. The procedure used to resolve this conflict contained two important elements: the disputants selected a third party to act as an umpire; and the decision made by the third party was accepted as binding.

In any conflict situation, the parties which are involved have three general options. First, they may choose to remain at loggerheads until one side forces the other to acquiesce. Second, they may decide to meet in private to negotiate a diplomatic settlement. Or, finally, they may seek to employ the assistance of some third party to help resolve their disagreement. Of course, there are many variations to each of these three options. Arbitration, for instance, is but one of several possible variations on the last option. As can be seen in the conflict between Lagash and Umma, arbitration is a means for settling disputes that allows the contestants to select a third party who, in turn, will make a binding judgement on the case in question. Thus, arbitration differs from third-party mediation because the decision made by the arbitrator is binding. On the other hand, it also differs from third-party adjudication because the dispute is not submitted to a standing court. Consequently, arbitration has traditionally been considered a potent but flexible technique for resolving conflicts.

The parties in an arbitration usually sign a preliminary agreement, or *compromis*, which specifies both the subject of the dispute and the procedures that will be followed in rendering a decision. As long as the third party does not stray from the terms set forth in the *compromis*, the parties are bound by the decision. According to Subbarao, there are four approaches which the third party may take in order to reach a decision once the arbitration machinery is set in motion:

1. Final-offer-selection. The arbitrator may base the award on one or the other parties' final package of offers.

2. Last-offer-by-issue. The arbitrator may base the award on one or the other parties' last offer on each separate issue.

3. Open-award. The arbitrator may give an award without any regard to the parties' final positions.

4. Compromise-award. the arbitrator may split the difference between the parties' final positions.[1]

Normally the *compromis* will outline the principles that are to guide the third party in his deliberations on the case. In recent years, arbitrators have been urged to reach their decisions "on the basis of respect for law."[2] While there is some disagreement over the utility of this guide,[3] it is generally regarded as a way to remove political considerations from the deliberative process.

Perhaps the main reason for the great stress given to the judicial character of arbitration lies in the premise that states resort to war whenever misconceptions, wounded sensibilities, and aroused national passions obscure alternative modes of redress. Hence it is assumed that third-party arbitration could prevent the outbreak of war because dispassionate intermediaries would bring the facts of a dispute to light and would propose a just solution. Moreover, an impartial third party offers a clear last chance to the disputants: "if agreement is badly desired and further negotiation out of the question, the arbitrator's suggestion may be accepted in default of any alternative."[4] As Randolph has put it, third-party procedures offer distinct advantages in each phase of the settlement process:

In the initial phase, parties can more readily agree on the third party than decide all important aspects of negotiating positions. . . . In the intermediate phase, third parties can propose solutions which parties find acceptable but cannot advance because of disadvantages for partial interests in taking on a moderate position. In the final phase, third parties can expect support from the public . . . in behalf of enforcement solutions, a support less freely extended to parties because of association with conflict and partial interests.[5]

In summary, arbitration is one of the most respected techniques of conflict resolution. It is mentioned more than three times as often as adjudication, and more than five times as often as mediation in the treaties registered with the United Nations from 1945 through 1965.[6] But even though it is held in high esteem, very few quantitative historical analyses of the type done on adjudication and mediation have been carried out on arbitration.[7]

Contending Interpretations of Arbitral Activity

The first step in undertaking any research endeavor is empirical description. Only after diachronic fluctuations in international arbitration have been systematically profiled will it be possible to analyze those factors which may account for their variation.[8] This mapping operation is particularly important in the light of the scholarly disagreement regarding longitudinal transformations in arbitral activity since the Congress of Vienna. As this sizable, albeit impressionistic, body of academic opinion has yet to be confronted with data, the following set of anatomical, first-order propositions has been abstracted from literature on post-1815 trends in international arbitration.[9] After discussing these propositions, data on various dimensions of arbitral activity will be utilized to evaluate their accuracy.

Proposition 1: Arbitral activity increased during the nineteenth century. "During the hundred years following the Jay Treaty," notes Larson, "there was a strong upsurge in the use of arbitration in international disputes."[10] Though not all observers concur with Nussbaum that this growth was a "remarkable phenomenon,"[11] there is agreement among international relations scholars and analysts of international law that a strong upward trend in the incidence of arbitration occurred during the nineteenth century.[12] Furthermore, as Read has pointed out, the tendency to regard arbitration as a desirable method for adjusting international disputes also became more pronounced in the last century.[13]

Proposition 2: The Alabama claims case initiated an upward trend in arbitral activity. A broad scholarly consensus likewise exists regarding the importance of the arbitrative settlement of U.S. claims that the United Kingdom had violated her neutrality by permitting the confederate privateer *Alabama* and its supply ship *Georgia* to be constructed in British shipyards.[14] "If the Jay Treaty of 1794 rescued arbitral process as a means of settling international disputes from desuetude," argue Simpson and Fox, then "the *Ala-*

bama claims arbitration . . . gave the process a new impetus. . . ."[15] It is thought that this momentum was induced by the utilization of a novel tribunal structure to successfully resolve conflict between what Fawcett called the "vital interests" of the two countries.[16] Under the 1871 Washington Treaty, each state appointed one member to the arbitral tribunal, and additional members were selected by the emperor of Brazil, king of Italy, and president of the Swiss Confederation. With the precedent of a collegiate international tribunal established, chroniclers of global norms generally conclude that arbitration "gained renewed prestige"[17] and widespread popularity.[18]

Proposition 3.1: The period between 1890 and 1910 constituted a turning point in arbitral activity.

Proposition 3.2: The period between 1890 and 1910 did not constitute a turning point in arbitral activity. Unlike the accord which characterized scholarly assessment of the *Alabama* claims arbitration, analyses of the 1890–1910 era are marked by divergence over the question of that period's criticality as a pivotal stage in the growth of international arbitration. Rhyne, for instance, emphasizes its significance by contending that the 1892 *Behring Sea Seal Fisheries* case "greatly enhanced the prestige of arbitration as an important method for the peaceful settlement of international disputes."[19] Read stresses the period's salience too, but claims that the "impetus to the negotiation of arbitration agreements was given by the establishment of the Permanent Court of Arbitration, by the First Hague Conference in 1899."[20] Tung amplifies this point by submitting that the Permanent Court of Arbitration "paved the way for further expansion of international arbitration. . . ."[21]

De Visscher gives an alternative interpretation. He notes that irrespective of the 1899 and 1907 Hague Conferences, the arbitral practice of states "showed hardly any change."[22]

The Hague Conferences certainly cannot be denied the merit of having surrounded arbitration with an atmosphere favorable to judicial settlement; but it must be admitted that, in the narrow confines to which it was restricted by the hostility of the Powers to the very principle of a serious arbitral obligation, international justice had no chance to contribute to the maintenance of peace.[23]

That is to say, although the Hague Conferences stimulated compulsory arbitration treaties, often they were limited by extensive reservations.[24] The 1903 agreement between Britain and France, for example, established the maxim that disputes affecting the independence, honor, or vital interests of states would not be considered justiciable. Similar formulas were included within successive treaties thus restricting the principle of compulsory arbitration. Hence, as Dickinson's portrayal of the 1910 *North Atlantic Coast Fisheries* case indicates, the period's arbitrations resulted in "no credit to judicial statecraft, and no contribution to much needed confidence in the process of arbitration."[25]

Proposition 4.1: Arbitral activity has increased during the twentieth century.

Proposition 4.2: Arbitral activity has decreased during the twentieth century. In addition to the controversy regarding the impact of the 1890–1910 period upon international arbitration, there is disagreement over whether twentieth-century arbitrations followed an upward or downward secular trend. On the one hand, it is asserted that the scope of international law has increased,[26] and the Permanent Court of Arbitration has made remarkable progress in applying this body of law.[27] On the other hand, many observers subscribe to Stone's view that "state willingness to accept third-party judgment has shown a distinct retrogression."[28] Jenks, for instance, sees a reduction in the volume of arbitral activity;[29] and Corbett insists that events such as the Kellogg-Briand Pact and the 1928 General Act for the Pacific Settlement of International Disputes did not actuate any subsequent increase.[30]

Proposition 5.1: Arbitral activity in the nineteenth and twentieth centuries primarily occurred in low-salience issue-areas.

Proposition 5.2: Arbitral activity pertaining to contractual issues has increased in the twentieth century.

Proposition 5.3: Arbitral activity pertaining to the treatment of individuals has increased in the twentieth century. One reason frequently given for the alleged decline in twentieth-century arbitral activity is the reluctance of states to employ third parties for adjudicating more than simple marginal matters.[31] Diplomats, it is argued, have been hesitant to establish which future conflicts will be thereafter considered justiciable, normally relying instead upon a *pactum de contrahendo* to provide the framework for later agreement. Yet, in the absence of any previous definition of justiciability, consent often has not been granted to arbitrate politically salient issues. "Among the twenty decisions rendered by the Permanent Court of Arbitration," attests Morgenthau, "there is none that can be called political. . . ."[32] Hence, Rosen and Jones posit that the acceptance of judicial settlement is a "function of subject matter."[33]

Some authors have voiced reservations about this view. Jacobini insists that certain arbitrations have dealt with serious affairs. Therefore he postulates that the "context of a controversy may be more the real question than the intrinsic importance of the specific issue in dispute."[34] Furthermore, Jessup professes that recently a greater number of arbitrations have been concluded in the areas of commerce and individual grievance.[35] But this increase may not reflect changes in the efficacy of arbitration as a mode of conflict resolution for, according to Coplin[36] and Zook,[37] arbitration is commonly used within issue-areas of high salience to formalize agreements which each party has already concluded.

Proposition 6: Tribunals were utilized more frequently than individuals as arbitrators during the nineteenth and twentieth centuries. A key feature in the process of international arbitration is the ability of claimants to select the arbitrator. Historically, arbitrators have ranged from individuals (e.g., the Pope, a head of state, diplomat, or jurist) to collegiate bodies. Except in the case of ancient Chinese interstate relations, Wright observes that governments have preferred to use tribunals to resolve their disputes.[38]

Measuring Arbitral Activity

The codification of international law has long been sought by advocates of world peace through arbitration. Yet, despite the many notable attempts to organize the principles found in historic legal cases into a coherent body of rules, researchers have been hesitant to convert the wealth of information about the cases themselves into quantitative data which could be used to test propositions regarding the causes and consequences of arbitration. What makes this demurrer remarkable is that meaning frequently is attached to numerical magnitudes in judicial decisions. As Rohn has pointed out, large numbers of treaties, precedents, and so on translate into legal importance. Nevertheless, the relevance of magnitudes:

has not been recognized as having *theoretical* significance for our understanding of international law as a whole. Therefore, there is no general inventory of quantifiable data in international law, comparable in dependability and sophistication to international trade statistics, international gold flow figures, foreign aid accounts, production and consumption indices, population growth rates and many other statistical data which allows us to measure and hence better understand other aspects of public life on our planet. In international law we have not even reached the point where we take it for granted that a basic inventory of facts and magnitudes is both necessary and available.[39]

Consequently, there are no existing studies which provide empirical evidence that would allow us to either accept or reject the theoretical propositions found in the literature on arbitration.

As a result of this situation, it was necessary to operationalize the concept of arbitral activity and then collect data for the spatio-temporal domain under study. Invariably students of political behavior ask three key questions when scrutinizing arbitrative settlements. First, how widespread was the phenomena? Second, which states were engaged in its practice? And third, what types of issues were arbitrated?

These queries suggested the need for variables which would measure different dimensions of arbitral activity. Toward this end, the following indices were constructed to probe the incidence of arbitration within what Singer has labeled as the "central system:"[40]

Scope—   the number of central system participants in arbitrative settlements as percentage of the total central system membership.

Amplitude— the number of major power arbitrations as a percentage of all central system arbitrations.

The raw data used in these indices were made from information contained in Stuyt's compilation of those international arbitrations which have occurred since the 1794 Jay Treaty.[41] While it is conceivable that some nineteenth- and twentieth-century arbitrations have never been made public and therefore the total universe of arbitrations is unknown, the list provided by Stuyt still constitutes a compilation sufficient to satisfy our research needs. Not only is it the most exhaustive and recently updated compendium in existence, but it also has been used successfully in the only other quantitative study of arbitration known to the author.[42]

The information in the Stuyt survey also furnished the ingredients for a third index of arbitral activity. In order to measure temporal variation in the kinds of issues which have been arbitrated, the raw data were coded on the basis of the issue-area typology suggested by Coplin and Rochester.[43] Four categories were used. Type 1 issues pertained to contractual obligations and pecuniary matters, plus disputes involving the interpretation, modification, or disposition of treaties, conventions, protocols, and other related agreements. Type 2 issues concerned the treatment of nationals, aliens, and minority groups (e.g., illegal arrests, arbitrary arrests, and the derogation of rights). Type 3 issues dealt with possessory and jurisdictional rights over territory, fisheries, and related subjects. Lastly, Type 4 issues included disputes arising from maritime seizures, confiscations and expropriations, plus questions resulting from insurrection, civil war, and military operations. Table 1.1 shows the resulting issue-area distribution of central system arbitrations across time.[44] Coplin and Rochester have argued that "broader and more powerful segments of the domestic political environment become mobilized" as one moves from categories 1 through 4, which in turn magnifies the issue significance "for the foreign policy decision maker and hence the national actor taken as a collectivity."[45] Assuming that this interpretation is warranted, the following index will be used to probe yet another facet of arbitral activity:

Intensity— the number of Type 4 issues arbitrated as a percentage of all central system arbitrations.

Table 1.1   Issue Distribution of Central System Arbitrations (percentage figures)

Diplomatic Period	Issue-Area				
	1	2	3	4	Total
1815–1821	56	11	22	11	100
1822–1847	54	8	15	23	100
1848–1870	37	19	19	26	100
1871–1889	19	5	34	42	100
1890–1917	39	8	21	32	100
1918–1944	48	8	13	31	100
1945–1969	46	0	39	15	100
Total	41%	8%	21%	30%	100%
N = 331					

Armed with quantitative data on these three variables, it is now possible to test propositions 1 through 6. Figure 1.1 shows the secular trends over the past century and a half in the scope, amplitude, and intensity of arbitral activity. These line graphs, as well as their associated descriptive statistics, give us an empirical basis on which we can judge the accuracy of the conventional wisdom about arbitration.

The most prevalent assertion found in the literature on international arbitration was that arbitral activity increased during the nineteenth century. This view (proposition 1) received only partial support from the data, that is, whereas the scope of arbitral activity climbed from the 1830s

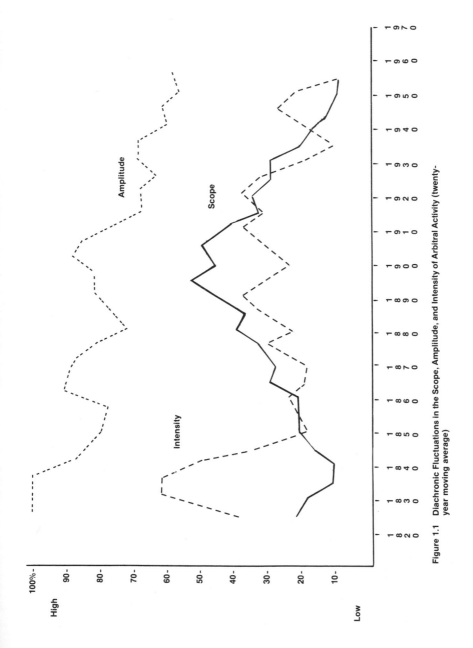

Figure 1.1 Diachronic Fluctuations in the Scope, Amplitude, and Intensity of Arbitral Activity (twenty-year moving average)

through the 1890s ($b = 1.74$), the intensity of arbitration did not show a consistent upward swing, and the amplitude of arbitration actually followed a downward trend ($b = -1.09$).

Despite claims in the literature to the contrary, not much of a case can be made for the historical periods which are usually considered breakpoints in these trends. For example, the *Alabama* claims case did not noticeably stimulate the growth rates for any of the three variables as predicted by proposition 2. Nor is the evidence conclusive for the 1890–1910 time frame. To be sure, the amplitude, scope, and subsequently even the intensity of arbitral activity did undergo change. But whereas supporters of proposition 3.1 predicted the change would result in an upturn in arbitral activity, the values of all three variables fell.

Unlike the nineteenth century, the direction of twentieth-century trends in arbitral activity did not vary from one dimension of behavior to the next. The values of all three variables displayed downward trends, with amplitude showing the smallest slope ($b = -1.98$) and scope showing the largest ($b = -3.85$). Given the common direction of these trends, we can reject proposition 4.1 in favor of its null counterpart.

Aside from focusing upon the trends and turning points in the amount of arbitral activity, the literature also contained observations about certain characteristics regarding the settlement procedure itself; e.g., the type of arbitrator utilized and the political importance of the issue arbitrated. The findings reported in Table 1.2 are consonant with proposition 5.1. Forty-one percent of the issues arbitrated betwen 1815 and 1969 fell under the Type 1 category—the least salient of the four issue-areas. Even when disaggregated into diplomatic eras, the tendency (except from 1871 to 1889) has been to arbitrate low-salience issues. Propositions 5.2 and 5.3, though, were not confirmed. The proportion of contractual issues arbitrated has remained relatively constant across time, and the percentage of arbitrations dealing with treatment of individuals has decreased. Again, the exception to both these generalizations was the 1871–1899 period.

Table 1.2   Type of Arbiter Selected in Central System Disputes, by Diplomatic Period (percentage figures)

Diplomatic Period	Individual Arbitrator	Arbitral Tribunal	Total
1815–1821	11	89	100
1822–1847	31	69	100
1848–1870	26	74	100
1871–1889	26	74	100
1890–1917	31	69	100
1918–1944	35	65	100
1945–1969	23	77	100
Total	30%	70%	100%
N = 331			

Finally, the empirical evidence strongly supported proposition 6. When the raw data were coded according to the type of arbitrator utilized, only thirty percent of the arbitrations since the Congress of Vienna were seen to have employed individual arbitrators. Furthermore, regardless of the diplomatic period analyzed, tribunals were clearly utilized more than individuals as the third-party to an arbitration. This finding is buttressed by the results reported in Table 1.3. That is to say, tribunals were selected more frequently than individuals in each issue-area, although the distribution was more equal in Type 2 arbitrations.

Table 1.3   Type of Arbiter Selected in Central System Disputes, by Issue Area (percentage figures)

Issue Area	Individual Arbitrator	Arbitral Tribunal	Total
1	24	76	100
2	42	58	100
3	29	71	100
4	35	65	100
Total	30%	70%	100%
N = 331			

In conclusion, the purpose of this chapter was to give a quantitative description of the pattern of arbitral activity during the nineteenth and twentieth centuries. We have seen that although the use of international arbitration has declined in recent years, there have been periods of time when numerous states have submitted rather important issues to third-party arbitration. What accounts for this phenomenon? Are certain systemic conditions associated with the use of arbitration? Having identified those first-order propositions which accurately describe the pattern of arbitral activity over the past two centuries, it is now possible to investigate those second-order propositions which purport to name the systemic correlates of this pattern.

Notes

1. A. V. Subbarao, "The Impact of Binding Interest Arbitration in Negotiation and Process Outcome," *Journal of Conflict Resolution* 22 (March 1978): 81. For a discussion of the procedural rules involved in the conduct of an international arbitration, see Kenneth S. Carlston, *The Process of International Arbitration* (New York: Columbia University Press, 1946), chaps. 1–2.

2. In contrast to this practice, arbitral proceedings in sub-Saharan Africa aim more at mutual accommodation than at rendering a decision which strictly complies with some objective norm. See Adda B. Bozeman, *Conflict in Africa, Concepts and Realities* (Princeton: Princeton University Press, 1976), pp. 237–38.

3. Bibó, for instance, has called for arbitration which is political "in the sense that its decisions are motivated by political judgments rather than through applying the rules of law or just clarifying facts." In his view, arbitrators "must weigh what is possible politically with what is correct conceptually in order . . . to find solutions that will be able to withstand foreseeable pressures and simultaneously represent the application and continuous development of principles." István Bibó, *The Paralysis of International Institutions and the Remedies: A Study of Self-Determination, Concord among the Major Powers, and Political Arbitration* (New York: Halsted Press, John Wiley & Sons, 1976), p. 135.

4. Thomas C. Schelling, *Arms and Influence* (New Haven: Yale University Press, 1966), p. 140. Also see Inis L. Claude, Jr., *Swords into Plowshares, The Problems and Progress of International Organization* 3rd ed. (New York: Random House, 1964), pp. 199–204.

5. Lillian Randolph, *Third Party Settlements of Disputes in Theory and Practice* (Dobbs Ferry, N.Y.: Oceana Publications, Inc., 1973), p. 2.

6. These figures are based on data in Curtis G. Reithel, "International

Dispute Settlement: An Analysis of Dispute Settlement Clauses in Treaties" (Paper presented at the 1976 annual meeting of the International Studies Association, Toronto, Canada, February 25-29, 1976), p. 15.

7. A representative sample of this literature would include William D. Coplin and J. Martin Rochester, "The Permanent Court of International Justice, the International Court of Justice, the League of Nations, and the United Nations: A Comparative Empirical Survey," *American Political Science Review* 66 (June 1972): 529-50; Daniel Frei, "Conditions Affecting the Effectiveness of International Mediation," *Peace Science Society (International) Papers* 26 (1976), pp. 67-84; K. J. Holsti, "Resolving International Conflicts: A Taxonomy of Behavior and Some Figures on Procedures," *Journal of Conflict Resolution* 10 (September 1966): 272-96; and Edward P. Levine, "Mediation in International Politics: A Universe and Some Observations," *Peace Research Society Papers* 17 (1971), pp. 23-43. Although there has not been much work of this kind on arbitration, a considerable amount of game theoretic research has been undertaken. See R. Duncan Luce and Howard Raiffa, *Games and Decisions* (New York: John Wiley & Sons, 1957), pp. 137-45.

8. Carl G. Hempel, in "Fundamentals of Concept Formation in Empirical Science," *International Encyclopedia of Unified Science*, Vol. 2 (Chicago: University of Chicago Press, 1952), p. 1, has asserted that a major objective of empirical science is "to describe particular phenomena in the world of our experience. . . ." Singer agrees and has forwarded an investigatory strategy based upon the premise that the existential knowledge resultant from description constitutes the "bedrock" without which "we cannot make predictions or explanations with any degree of confidence." J. David Singer, *The Scientific Study of Politics: An Approach to Foreign Policy Analysis* (Morristown, N.J.: General Learning Press, 1972), p. 5.

9. Anatomical propositions are existential statements which describe the characteristics of a concept at a specific point in time, or the periodicities and secular trend in the incidence of that concept across time. In contrast, bivariate (i.e., second-order) propositions are relational statements which specify the association between two concepts. James G. March and Herbert A. Simon, *Organizations* (New York: John Wiley & Sons, 1958), p. 8.

10. Arthur Larson, *When Nations Disagree* (Baton Rouge, La.: Louisiana State University Press, 1961), p. 66.

11. Arthur Nussbaum, *A Concise History of the Law of Nations* (New York: Macmillan, 1947), p. 66.

12. For example, see respectively C. Wilfred Jenks, *Law in the World Community* (New York: David McKay Company, Inc., 1967), p. 10; and Frederick H. Hartmann, *The Relations of Nations* 2nd ed. (New York: Macmillan Co., 1957), p. 119.

13. Elizabeth F. Read, *International Law and International Relations* (New York: American Foundation, Inc., 1925), pp. 105-6.

14. For a representative sample of literature reflecting this opinion, see Norman D. Palmer and Howard C. Perkins, *International Relations, The World Community in Transition* 3rd ed. (Boston: Houghton Mifflin Co.,

1969), p. 259; Charles P. Schleicher, *International Relations, Cooperation and Conflict* (Englewood Cliffs, N.J.: Prentice-Hall, 1954), p. 220; and Walter R. Sharp and Grayson Kirk, *Contemporary International Politics* (New York: Rinehart & Company, 1940), p. 458.

15. J. L. Simpson and Hazel Fox, *International Arbitration, Law and Practice* (New York: Frederick A. Praeger, 1959), p. 8.

16. J. E. S. Fawcett, *The Law of Nations* (New York: Basic Books, 1968), p. 21.

17. Kurt von Schuschnigg, *International Law: An Introduction to the Law of Peace* (Milwaukee: Bruce Publishing Company, 1959), p. 298.

18. Ian Brownlie, *Principles of Public International Law* 2nd ed. (Oxford: Clarendon Press, 1973), p. 684.

19. Charles S. Rhyne, *International Law* (Washington, D.C.: C.L.B. Publishers, 1971), p. 17.

20. Read, *International Law*, p. 115.

21. William L. Tung, *International Law in an Organizing World* (New York: Thomas Y. Crowell Company, 1968), p. 27.

22. Charles De Visscher, *Theory and Reality in Public International Law* rev. ed., trans. P. E. Corbett (Princeton: Princeton University Press, 1968), p. 360.

23. Ibid., p. 50.

24. Quincy Wright, *Contemporary International Law: A Balance Sheet* (Garden City, N.Y.: Doubleday & Company, 1955), p. 34.

25. Edwin D. Dickinson, *Law and Peace* (Philadelphia: University of Pennsylvania Press, 1951), p. 85.

26. Wolfgang Friedman, *The Changing Structure of International Law* (New York: Columbia University Press, 1964), p. 71.

27. G. W. Mangone, *A Short History of International Organization* (New York: McGraw-Hill, 1954), p. 138.

28. Julius Stone, "The International Court and World Crisis," *International Conciliation* (January 1962): 31.

29. Jenks, *World Community*, p. 10.

30. Percey E. Corbett, *The Growth of World Law* (Princeton: Princeton University Press, 1971), p. 40.

31. Endorsement of this perspective can be found in such diverse works as J. L. Brierly, *The Basis of Obligation in International Law*, ed. H. Lauterpacht (Oxford: Clarendon Press, 1958), p. 93; Ivo D. Duchacek, *Nations and Men* 2nd ed. (New York: Holt, Rinehart and Winston, 1968), p. 519; and Morton A. Kaplan and Nicholas deB. Katzenbach, *The Political Foundations of International Law* (New York: John Wiley & Sons, 1961), p. 275.

32. Hans J. Morgenthau, *Politics Among Nations, The Struggle for Power and Peace* 3rd ed. (New York: Alfred A. Knopf, 1966), p. 432.

33. Steven Rosen and Walter Jones, *The Logic of International Relations* (Cambridge, Mass.: Winthrop Publishers, 1974), p. 277.

34. H. B. Jacobini, *International Law: A Text* (Homewood, Ill.: Dorsey Press, 1962), p. 201.

35. Phillip C. Jessup, *A Modern Law of Nations* (New York: Macmillan Co. Archon Books, 1968), pp. 95, 141.

36. William D. Coplin, *The Function of International Law* (Chicago: Rand McNally, 1966), p. 79.

37. David H. Zook, Jr., *The Conduct of the Chaco War* (New York: Bookman Associates, 1960).

38. Quincy Wright, "Asian Experience and International Law," *International Studies 1* (July 1959): 80. *The Role of International Law in the Elimination of War* (Manchester: Manchester University Press, 1961), p. 79.

39. Peter H. Rohn, *Treaty Profiles* (Santa Barbara, Cal.: Clio Press, 1976), p. 8. Emphasis added.

40. Because international law is often said to be a product of the most active and influential states within international affairs, the central system was used as the spatial domain for this study. For a discussion of the composition and membership criteria, see J. David Singer and Melvin Small, *The Wages of War 1816-1965: A Statistical Handbook* (New York: John Wiley & Sons, 1972), pp. 19-30.

41. A. M. Stuyt, *Survey of International Arbitrations, 1794-1970* (Leiden, The Netherlands: A. W. Sijthoff, 1972).

42. Michael Mihalka, "Realpolitik, Arbitrations, and the Use of Force: The European Experience 1816-1970," *Peace Science Society (International) Papers* 27 (1977), pp. 77-87.

43. Coplin and Rochester, "The Permanent Court of International Justice," p. 542. The major difference between their typology and the one used here lies in our collapsing of threatened and actual hostilities into one category; i.e., Type 4 issues.

44. The diplomatic period delineated in Table 1.1 (and throughout this chapter) are derived from Richard N. Rosecrance, *Action and Reaction in World Politics* (Boston: Little, Brown and Company, 1963).

45. Coplin and Rochester, "The Permanent Court of International Justice," p. 542.

CHAPTER 2

Identifying the Normative Correlates of Arbitral Activity

Force and not opinion is queen of the world;
but it is opinion that uses force.

—Pascal

An Approach to Conceptualizing the Cultural Attributes of the International System

In Voltaire's novelette *Micromégas*, the earth is visited by a gigantic extraterrestrial being. While wading through the Mediterranean, the curious visitor plucks a nearby ship from the sea, causing confusion and turmoil among its passengers: "The chaplains of the ship repeated exorcisms, the sailors swore, and the philosophers formed a system" to explain the bewildering occurrence. Confronted with the formidable task of explaining global interactions, many international relations theorists have also attempted to make sense out of the bewildering events which they observe by viewing them from a systems perspective.

Analytically, the international system may be thought of as an aggregation of interdependent entities that contains three basic characteristics: cultural attributes, structural attributes, and behavioral patterns. In the preceding chapter, the pattern of arbitral behavior between 1815 and 1969 was described. The next two chapters will examine changes in those cultural and structural attributes of the international system which have covaried with fluctuations in arbitral activity.

Let us begin with the cultural attributes. The orthodox view of world politics is based on the twin pillars of state sovereignty and international anarchy. But as Masters reminds us, "if we speak of international 'anarchy,' it would be well to bear in mind that it is an 'ordered anarchy.'"[1] In other words, there are a number of regulatory mechanisms operative in the international system which mitigate conflict and lend a modicum of predictability to the relations between states.

One of these mechanisms is a framework of collective expectations provided by legal norms. For the purposes of this study, legal norms will be conceptualized as an expression of prevailing attitudes about the state system; that is, as statements communicating those beliefs which members of the system generally hold about specific types of behavior. When legal norms are conceived of in this way, several theoretical assumptions are made about the cultural attributes of the international system. The most elementary of these is that although there are various sources of international law (e.g., treaties), these materials ultimately reflect a changeable body of quasi-authoritative guides, known in juristic literature as legal norms.[2]

The second assumption is that although legal norms are multifunctional, it is possible to examine any given function independently of the others. According to Hoebel, one of the primary tasks of law is to define relationships among society's members.[3] By focusing on communication, this study accepts Coplin's argument that legal norms operate "on the level of the individual's perceptions and attitudes by presenting him with an image of the social system—an image which has both factual and normative aspects and which contributes to social order by building a consensus on procedural as well as on substantive matters."[4]

From this a third assumption follows. Although norms can be defined and classified in many ways, it is useful to view them as beliefs which provide group members with a shared frame of reference.[5] As Willhelm puts it, norms are "standards *for* social conduct; they are guides that direct the expression of social behavior. As such, norms are not equivalent to conduct; norms are constructs for analyzing social action rather than facets of social behavior."[6]

The last assumption is that although the international political culture is shaped by an individual's subjective orientations toward political objects, it nonetheless may be analyzed from a macro perspective. Strictly speaking, when an individual thinks, he "finds himself in an inherited situation with patterns of thought . . . and attempts to elaborate further the inherited modes of response or to substitute others for them."[7] Seen in this light, the cultural attributes of the international system may be said to possess a set of linked norms which contain those legal symbols used to communicate modal patterns of thought about the behavior which ought to be followed by national actors in particular situations.

Changing Attitudes toward the Use of Force

To conceptualize international norms as a medium for communication is to stress the role of legal symbols in diplomatic bargaining. The essential features of a bargaining situation exist if:

1. Both parties perceive that there is the possibility of reaching an agreement in which each party would be better off, or no worse off, than if no agreement is reached.
2. Both parties perceive that there is more than one such agreement which could be reached.

3. Both parties perceive each other to have conflicting preferences or opposed interests with regard to the different agreements which might be reached.[8]

When societal complexity precludes the use of tacit coordination to find focal point solutions for these mixed-motive situations, Barkun asserts that the disputants will often bring a third party into the bargaining process. "Societal complexity," he writes, "requires symbolic complexity so that the societal complexity can be understood, but complex symbols beget complex and unsure meanings."[9] Hence the third party acquires the task of drawing inferences from those legal symbols which define a situation. Thus it is not surprising that Rapoport has concluded that no sharp distinction can be drawn between bargaining and arbitration.[10]

Among the most important legal norms which influence international bargaining are those that pertain to the use of force. During the past century and a half there has been considerable change in the content of these norms, although scholars differ over the direction of the change and precisely when it occurred. Listed below are a group of anatomical propositions reflecting this disagreement. After briefly discussing each proposition, time-series data will be marshaled to test their accuracy. The results from this graphic analysis will also be used to see whether changes in these norms are associated in any way with trends in the scope, amplitude, or intensity of arbitral activity.

Proposition 7: The resort to war was recognized as a legal instrument of statecraft during the nineteenth century.

Proposition 8.1: The resort to war has been recognized as a legal instrument of statecraft during the twentieth century.

Proposition 8.2: The resort to war has not been recognized as a legal instrument of statecraft during the twentieth century. Although most observers do not agree on whether legal norms can deter war, they concur that war was considered an acceptable foreign policy tool prior to the outbreak of World War I.[11] Two corollaries follow this assertion. First, since international law did not restrict states from resorting to war, it purported instead to limit the uses of force short of war.[12] Second, whereas statesmen did not accept any differentiation between those circumstances under which war was permissible and those under which it was not, reciprocal rules were formed to govern the treatment of prisoners, the wounded, and neutrals.[13] In short, judicial positivism of nineteenth century international law agreed with Clausewitz that war was a continuation of foreign policy by other means, and therefore the law sought only to regulate the conduct of military operations without judging the rationale for resorting to arms.

The prevailing interpretation of twentieth century attitudes toward the use of force is that war no longer remains *zweckrational*. It is argued that the Kellog-Briand Pact, the Geneva Protocol, and the 1933 Antiwar Treaty of Rio de Janeiro all reflect a vast transformation in global beliefs. That is, rather than focusing upon the regulation of war, emphasis now resides in its prevention. In contrast to the nineteenth century, however, not all investigators subscribe to one viewpoint. In the first place, controversy abounds over the issue of periodization: some writers contend that this attitudinal metamorphosis took place in the aftermath of World War I,[14] while others profess that its roots reach back to the earlier Hague Conferences.[15] In the second place, questions have been raised about the degree of change in sentiments regarding war. For instance, Steiner[16] submits that the laws of war collapsed with the advent of Ludendorff's conception of *Der totale Krieg*, but Aron[17] suggests that since not all wars were prohibited in the League Covenant, perhaps the outlook toward the use of force was not so drastically altered as many suppose. Thus in reviewing the literature dealing with perceptions of the legality of war, one finds a consensus that war was condoned in the nineteenth century, but disagreement over whether legal norms condemned its use after the turn of the century.

Proposition 9.1: The importance of military necessity as a reason for initiating conflict increased in the nineteenth century.

Proposition 9.2: The importance of the just war concept as a reason for initiating conflict did not increase until after World War I. The doctrine of *raison d'état* accompanied nineteenth-century notions about the instrumental value of war. Under its province, war became more a question of necessity than choice.[18] Consequently, traditional limitations upon the use of force inherent in the long-standing idea of the *bellum iustum* were disregarded because "acceptance of auto-interpretation effectively allowed each belligerant to attribute justice to his own use of force. . . ."[19] The standard image of nineteenth-century norms posits that as the principle of military necessity grew in popularity, "the just-war concept was submerged, making only occasional reappearances in legal doctrine."[20] Alternatively, the twentieth-century image portrays the opposite situation: *Kriegsraison* was condemned at the Nuremberg trials, while the notion of just war was resurrected at Versailles and flourished in the wake of Hiroshima.[21] Notwithstanding the recent debate as to whether this implies that legal norms currently accept preventive wars[22] and "wars of liberation,"[23] the preceding considerations lead one to hypothesize with Sterling that an inverse relationship exists between trends in the prominence of military necessity and the just war doctrine.[24]

Proposition 10: The importance of norms regarding the rights and duties of neutrals increased during the nineteenth century.

Proposition 11.1: The importance of norms regarding the rights and duties of neutrals increased during the twentieth century.

Proposition 11.2: The importance of norms regarding the rights and duties of neutrals decreased during the twentieth century.

Proposition 11.3: The importance of norms regarding the rights and duties of neutrals followed a cyclical pattern in the twentieth century. The laws of neutrality comprise a second product of nineteenth-century beliefs about recourse to war as a necessary element of sovereignty. If states were not obliged to judge the legitimacy of a conflict, then it was felt that the scope of warfare could be limited through the resulting impartiality of third parties. Obviously, rules governing the relations between neutrals and belligerents were needed to maintain this modus vivendi. According to Fenwick, following the armed neutralities initiated by Catherine the Great of Russia, these norms "won an equal position with the claims of belligerency," although specific "rights and duties were still lacking definition and precision."[25] Tung agrees, but adds that during the nineteenth century "neutrality as a legal institution *gradually* received recognition."[26] Hence by the end of the century, the "principle of the inviolability of neutral territory, and the neutral State's corresponding obligation to prevent belligerent use of its territory, acquired . . . a precision and firmness that they had long lacked."[27]

In contrast to the scholarly consensus one finds regarding the nineteenth century, considerable disagreement exists over the question as to whether norms bearing upon neutrality have continued to be operative since the end of World War I. At one extreme are those who believe so;[28] at the other extreme are those who insist that neutrality is now of little consequence.[29] Many reasons are given for this alleged retrogression, and that which this group voices most often is based upon the contemporary acceptance of collective security and the just war doctrine. From their vantage point, neutrality is philosophically incompatible with beliefs in common concern and the indivisibility of peace; therefore norms related to neutrality have decayed throughout this century.[30] Finally, midway between these poles it is possible to discern still another perspective. Representatives of this viewpoint suggest that the attention given to neutrality was absymally low by the time Manchuria was invaded, but began to rise when the Scandinavian Rules of Neutrality were adopted in 1938.[31] In sum, irrespective of widespread agreement on the evolution of neutrality directly following the Napoleonic era, serious divergences abound in judgmental assessments of contemporary neutrality norms.

Proposition 12.1: The importance of norms regarding the conduct of maritime war increased after the mid-nineteenth century.

Proposition 12.2: The importance of norms regarding the conduct of maritime war followed a cyclical pattern after the mid-nineteenth century. Maritime law represents a third outgrowth of nineteenth-century assumptions about the use of force. Not only was freedom of the seas deemed necessary for commercial expansion, preserving neutral trade, and acquiring additional territory, but it was also considered a requisite for security purposes. Most commentators agree with Oppenheim's observation that the attention devoted to laws of the high seas dramatically increased after the Crimean War, but they difer on what importance these legal norms had immediately thereafter.[32] Some writers point to the 1856 Declaration of Paris and the Geneva Convention of 1868 as evidence of an upward secular trend. Indeed, De Visscher claims that the area of maritime war contained the "greatest progress in international law."[33] Nonetheless other analysts of the period see notable periodicities in the significance attached to these norms. Hoffmann[34] finds signs of deterioration at the turn of the century, while Corbett[35] uncovers traces of an upswing in rules on submarine warfare thirty years later. A comparison of this assessment with our earlier delineation of the perceived salience of neutrality norms suggests that the conventional wisdom postulates a direct positive relationship between these two dimensions of the international legal system.

Proposition 13.1: There is an inverse relationship between the perceived importance of norms regarding the use of force and the perceived importance of arbitration.

Proposition 13.2: There is a direct relationship between the perceived importance of arbitration and the amount of arbitral activity within the international system. As can be seen above, most scholars support the thesis that nineteenth-century legal norms endorsed the sovereign prerogative to utilize force as a tool of statecraft. Moreover, they concur in the opinion that this attitude was reinforced by a widespread acceptance of military necessity as a legitimate guide and the attention given to the laws of neutrality and maritime war. Where they disagree is over their evaluation of whether the importance of these norms increased, decreased, or moved in a cyclical pattern during the twentieth century. Regardless of the pattern that occurred, the literature suggests that whenever force declines as an acceptable mode of dispute settlement, the perceived salience of arbitration and other amicable procedures increases. Furthermore, these upswings are thought to be directly related to increases in arbitral activity.

Monitoring Transformations in Attitudes toward the Use of Force

It is evident from these propositions that while a considerable amount has been written about the growth and decay of legal norms, little has been done to actually measure their change over time. No doubt much of this can be attributed to the fact that scholars have been hesitant to proceed in this direction without first knowing the real essence of law. Unfortunately, the essentialists who set out to find the true meaning of law face "a question upon which whole libraries have been written, and written, as their very existence shows, without definite results being attained."[36] Tempting as it may be to build one's work on real definitions, it is unlikely that such a foundation can be established given the open texture of the term in question and the numerous conflicting interpretations given the notions of truth and meaning. Thus as Nadar[37] suggests, rather than struggling to determine the real essence of law, it is more useful to ask: How might legal norms be conceptualized for research purposes?

If legal norms are conceptualized as quasi-authoritative statements which communicate prevailing assumptions about the state system, then one way to obtain information indirectly on these phenomena would be to examine something that was explicitly designed to portray the climate of opinion which existed at a particular point in history. The writings of eminent publicists constitute such an informational source. Although one could find other sources of information about which norms held sway during a specific

Table 2.1 A List of the Cultural Attributes under Investigation

Concept	Variable	Indicator	Abbreviation	Data Source
Forcible procedures of dispute settlement	Military necessity	Each publicist's judgment of the importance of the military necessity concept was coded on an ordinal continuum from 1 (low) to 5 (high).	NEC	Transnational Rules Indicator Project (TRIP)
	Just war	Each publicist's judgment of the importance of just war was coded on the following basis: (1) no mention of the doctrine, (2) doctrine discussed but not accepted, (3) doctrine accepted in the case of defensive wars, (4) doctrine accepted for defensive and preventive wars, and (5) doctrine accepted for offensive as well as defensive and preventive wars.	JUST	TRIP
	Maritime war	The amount of textual space alloted to maritime war by each publicist taken as a percentage of the total space devoted to all types of warfare.	MAR	TRIP
Forcible procedures falling short of war	Reprisal	The amount of textual space allotted to reprisal by each publicist taken as a percentage of the total space devoted to all types of nonamicable methods of redress.	REP	TRIP

	Description		
Retortion	The amount of textual space allotted to retortion by each publicist taken as a percentage of the total space devoted to all types of nonamicable methods of redress.	RET	TRIP
Pacific settlement procedures	The amount of textual space allotted to arbitration by each publicist taken as a percentage of the total space devoted to all pacific settlement procedures.	SAL	TRIP
	The amount of textual space allotted to mediation and conciliation by each publicist taken as a percentage of the total space devoted to all pacific settlement procedures.	NBDG	TRIP
Nonparticipation in disputes	The amount of textual space allotted to neutrality taken as a percentage of the total textual space.	NEU	TRIP

NOTE: Once individual scores were obtained from every treatise on these indicators, the mean score was calculated for each half-decade between 1815 and 1969.

time span (e.g., diplomatic memoirs), the opinions expressed by publicists in their treatises are especially well suited for data-making purposes since judicial tribunals have long considered them to be a source of "trustworthy evidence" about the norms operative in the international system at the time they were written.[38] By treating publicists as expert observers who describe the importance attributed to various legal norms, it becomes possible to derive data on changing attitudes toward particular norms through a content analysis and comparison of the various legal texts that were written over an extended time period. As Holsti points out, content analysis is a data-making procedure which may be performed upon any communication, "novel, newspaper, love song, diary, diplomatic note, poem, transcribed psychiatric review, and the like."[39] Moreover, it may be utilized to "draw inferences other than those concerning the characteristics of authors."[40] While it may be argued that the publicist's interpretation of legal norms is artifactual and plays only a nominal role in developing law, the concern here is not with delineating the formal content of international law, but rather with tracing changes in those attitudes which reflect the cultural attributes of the international system.

In order to accomplish this research task, 202 basic legal treatises were content analyzed under the auspices of the Transnational Rules Indicators Project (TRIP).[41] The criteria used to select the treatises centered on whether a work had gone through multiple revised editions, or had been identified as authoritative by either independent scholarship (e.g., listed in the Association of Law Schools' bibliography of international law texts) or by a recognized legal body such as the World Court. Table 2.1 lists the variables from the TRIP data set which were used to test propositions 7 through 13.

The most prevalent assertion found in literature on the use of force revealed that war was recognized as a legal instrument of statecraft prior to 1914. To analyze this assertion each treatise in the data set was coded according to its evaluation of the functions of war and the laws of war. The results which appear in Table 2.2 clearly uphold proposition 7. Ninety-five percent of the authors in the 1815–1914 ·

Table 2.2 The Distribution of Publicist Opinion Regarding the Legality and Control of War (percentage figures)

Attitudes toward the legality of war	1815–1914	1915–1974
An acceptable tool of foreign policy	47	21
An acceptable tool which is deficient in some areas	25	24
A legitimate mode of conflict resolution whose destructive effects should be limited	23	25
An illegitimate tool of foreign policy	5	30
Total	100%	100%

Attitudes toward the function of laws of war	1815–1914	1915–1974
Relevant to the elimination of interstate violence	8	25
Irrelevant to the initiation of armed hostilities, but relevant to the limitation of war's destructiveness	92	75
Total	100%	100%

period condoned the resort to war, and ninety-two percent maintained that the laws of war were irrelevant to the initiation of armed hostilities. Despite this finding, little support was marshaled for the corollary view that the legal attention given various nonamicable modes of redress substantially increased throughout this era. The line graph in Figure 2.1 shows that the importance of both retorsion (the legal use of force in retaliation for unfriendly acts by another state) and reprisals (the legal use of force in retaliation for the illegal acts of others) actually declined until mid-century.

The data likewise appear at variance with standard interpretations of post-1915 beliefs about nonamicable dispute settlement procedures. Despite an initial decline in the retorsion and reprisal indicators, the perceived importance of both uses of force increased after World War II. Nevertheless, a conspicuous shift in attitudes toward war can still be seen in Table 2.2. Hence the decision to reject proposition 8.1 and accept 8.2 seems warranted.

Turning to the next set of propositions, the line graph in

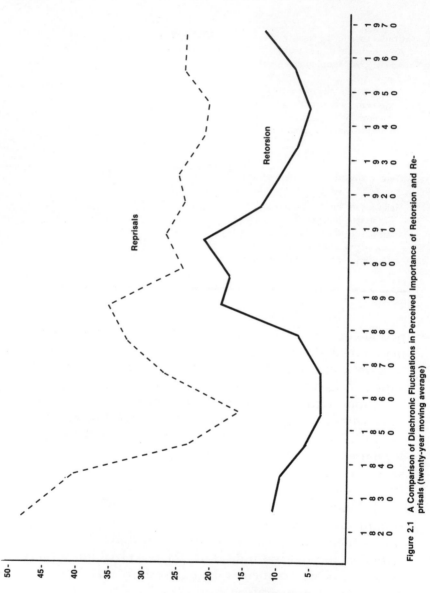

Figure 2.1   A Comparison of Diachronic Fluctuations in Perceived Importance of Retorsion and Reprisals (twenty-year moving average)

Figure 2.2 establishes that proposition 9.1 is correct in maintaining that the notion of military necessity was perceived to be quite important throughout the nineteenth century. But contrary to proposition 9.2, the just war doctrine grew in prominence several decades before the turn of the century, although it experienced a moderate drop in importance immediately prior to its upswing after World War II. When the trend lines for both military necessity and just war are compared, it becomes evident that the two variables do not show a strong inverse relationship as originally suspected.

Nor is the hypothesized relationship between the laws of neutrality and maritime war any more clear-cut. Figure 2.3 reveals that proposition 10 is correct in its description of the nineteenth-century growth in neutrality norms ($b = .97$), and it also demonstrates that proposition 11.2 accurately portrays their ensuing decay ($b = -1.50$). In contrast, Figure 2.4 discloses major shortcoming in the conventional wisdom regarding the perceived salience of legal norms relevant to maritime warfare. Not only does the attention devoted to these norms increase sooner than claimed by proposition 12.1, but the periodicities in these beliefs do not correspond precisely with those alluded to in proposition 12.2. Furthermore, when temporal variations in the perceived importance of neutrality and the laws of maritime war are compared, we find that the presumed positive relationship does not exist uniformly over time.

Moving finally to the last two propositions discussed in this chapter, the trend lines reported in Figure 2.5 show that the salience of arbitration as a dispute settlement technique rapidly increased ($b = 4.82$) during the second half of the nineteenth century. Even though its perceived importance fell in the twentieth century ($b = -1.43$), arbitration still retained greater favor in the eyes of legal scholars than nonbinding settlement procedures. Proposition 13.1 suggests that changes in the arbitration trend line are inversely related to changes in the importance of those norms which pertain to forcible techniques of dispute settlement. However, a comparison of Figure 2.5 with Figures 2.1–2.4 discloses that the only association which can be found concerns the perceived importance of neutrality.

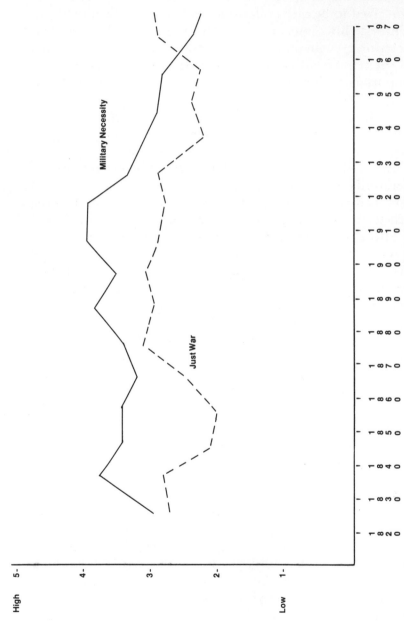

Figure 2.2 A Comparison of Diachronic Fluctuations in the Perceived Importance of Military Necessity and the Just War Doctrine (ten-year moving average)

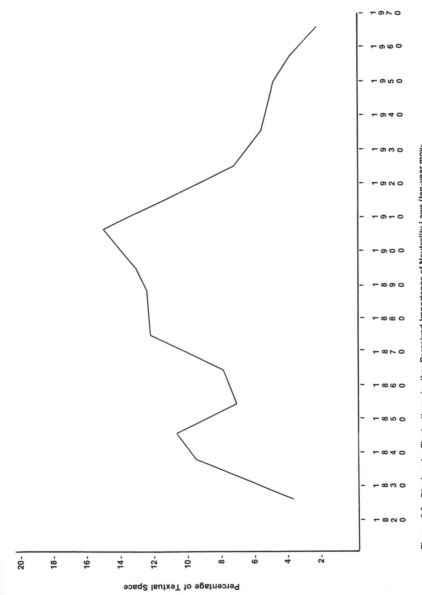

Figure 2.3 Diachronic Fluctuations in the Perceived Importance of Neutrality Laws (ten-year moving average)

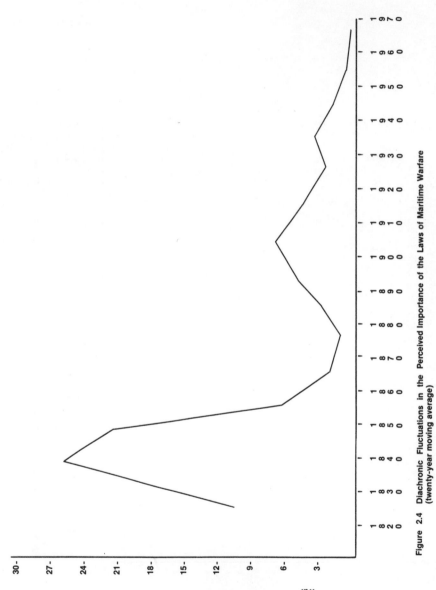

Figure 2.4   Diachronic Fluctuations in the Perceived Importance of the Laws of Maritime Warfare (twenty-year moving average)

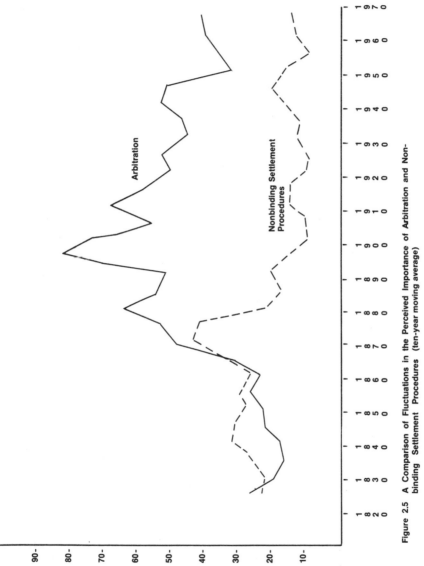

Figure 2.5   A Comparison of Fluctuations in the Perceived Importance of Arbitration and Non-binding Settlement Procedures   (ten-year moving average)

The evidence in support of proposition 13.2 is much stronger. When Figure 1.1 is compared with Figure 2.5 it appears that there is a positive relationship between the perceived salience of arbitration and the scope of arbitral activity. However, the results are less conclusive when the other two dimensions of the international arbitration are examined. While the perceived salience of arbitration seems to be directly related to the amplitude of arbitral activity in the twentieth century, the relationship between perceived salience and intensity is less clear. Consequently, the perceived salience of arbitration (SAL) will be included within a larger multivariate model of the determinants of arbitral activity in order to conduct further tests of its explanatory power.

This chapter has concentrated on three issues: changes in attitudes toward the use of force; the association between these changes and fluctuations in attitudes toward arbitration; and the relationship between the perceived importance of arbitration and the scope, amplitude, and intensity of arbitral activity. As stated earlier, cultural attributes comprise only part of our analytic framework. A complete presentation of the determinants of arbitral activity necessarily includes variables which also represent the structural attributes of the international system. The next chapter will examine the relationship between system structure and arbitral activity.

Notes

1. Roger D. Masters, "World Politics as a Primitive Political System," in *International Politics and Foreign Policy*, ed. James N. Rosenau (New York: Free Press, 1969), p. 112. The traditional perspective on international politics is analyzed in Arend Lijphard, "The Structure of the Theoretical Revolution in International Relations," *International Studies Quarterly* 17 (March 1974): 41-74.

2. This is not intended to imply that such standards of conduct do not have "fuzzy edges." To quote Lissitzyn, "legal standards even when they are called 'principles,' have fuzzy edges. There is always room for refinement and adjustment. In international law, however, the fuzziness of edges is probably greater than in most other sources of law." Oliver T. Lissitzyn, *The International Court of Justice* (New York: Carnegie Endowment for Peace, 1951), p. 8.

3. E. Adamson Hoebel, *The Law of Primitive Man* (Cambridge: Harvard University Press, 1961), chap. 2. See K. N. Llewellyn and E. Adamson Hoebel, *The Cheyenne Way: Conflict and Case Law in Primitive Jurisprudence* (Norman, Okla.: University of Oklahoma Press, 1941).

4. William D. Coplin, "International Law and Assumptions About the State System," *World Politics* 17 (July 1965): 617.

5. For a sample of the various meanings attributed to the term "norm," see Ragmar Rommetveit, *Social Norms and Roles* (Minneapolis: University of Minnesota Press, 1955), pp. 18–26; Muzafer Sherif, *The Psychology of Social Norms* (New York: Harper & Brothers, 1936), p. 3; and Georg Henrik von Wright, *Norm and Action, A Logical Inquiry* (London: Routledge & Kegan Paul, 1963), chap. 1. Examples of the many classificatory schemes include Richard T. Morris, "A Typology of Norms," *American Sociological Review* 21 (October 1956): 610–13; and the following works by Jack P. Gibbs: "Norms: The Problem of Definition and Classification," *American Journal of Sociology* 70 (March 1975): 586–94; and "The Sociology of Law and Normative Phenomena," *American Sociological Review* 31 (June 1966): 315–23. The antecedents of the conceptualization used here may be seen in G. C. Homans, *The Human Group* (New York: Harcourt Brace, 1950), p. 123; Kenneth E. Boulding, *The Image* (Ann Arbor: University of Michigan Press, 1956), pp. 57, 132; and Joseph E. McGrath, *Social Psychology* (New York: Holt, Rinehart and Winston, 1964), p. 105.

6. Sidney M. Willhelm, "A Reformulation of Social Action Theory," *American Journal of Economics and Sociology* (January 1967), p. 24.

7. Karl Mannheim, *Ideology and Utopia* (New York: Harcourt, Brace & World, 1936), p. 3.

8. Morton Deutsch and Robert M. Krauss, "Studies of Interpersonal Bargaining," in *Game Theory and Related Approaches to Social Behavior*, ed. Martin Shubik (New York: John Wiley & Sons, 1964), p. 325.

9. Michael Barkun, *Law Without Sanctions: Order in Primitive Societies and the World Community* (New Haven: Yale University Press, 1968), p. 121.

10. Anatol Rapoport, *Two-Person Game Theory* (Ann Arbor: University of Michigan Press, 1966), p. 216n. For an elaboration, see his *Strategy and Conscience* (New York: Schocken Books, 1964), chap. 7.

11. This convergence is evident in both international law and international relations texts. See H. B. Jacobini, *International Law: A Text* (Homewood, Ill.: Dorsey Press, 1962), p. 228; and C. P. Schleicher, *International Relations, Cooperation and Conflict* (Englewood Cliffs, N.J.: Prentice-Hall, 1962), p. 278.

12. J. L. Brierly, *The Law of Nations*, 6th ed. (New York: Oxford University Press, 1963), p. 398; Oliver J. Lissitzyn, *International Law Today and Tomorrow* (Dobbs Ferry, N.Y.: Oceana Press, 1965), p. 30.

13. T. Mathisen, *Methodology in the Study of International Relations* (New York: Macmillan, 1959), p. 110. Although the foundations for a *ius in bello* may be traced to the 1386 Ordinance of Richard II of England, the mid-nineteenth century generally is interpreted as a watershed in the

growth of laws aimed at humanizing warfare. George Schwarzenberger, *A Manual of International Law* 4th ed. (New York: Praeger Publishers, 1960), p. 188. In this regard, historians frequently point to the 1862 publication of Henri Dumant's eyewitness account of the Battle of Solferino, and the appearance a year later of Lieber's "Instructions for the Government of the Armies of the United States in the Field" as works which had a profound impact upon this trend. Other events which are often cited as evidence of increased concern include the 1864 Geneva Convention, the 1868 Declaration of St. Petersburg, the Brussels Conference of 1874, and the preparation shortly thereafter of the *Manuel de Lois de la Guerre Sur Terre* by the Institute of International Law.

14. For example, see Percy E. Corbett, *The Growth of World Law* (Princeton: Princeton University Press, 1971), p. 38; or Pitman B. Potter, *A Manual Digest of Common International Law* (New York: Harper and Brothers, 1932), p. 339.

15. See Qunicy Wright, *The Study of International Relations* (New York: Appleton-Century-Crofts, 1955), pp. 228-29.

16. H. A. Steiner, *Principles and Problems of International Relations* (New York: Harper and Brothers, 1940), p. 215.

17. Raymond Aron, *Peace and War, A Theory of International Relations*, trans. R. H. and A. B. Fox (New York: F. A. Praeger, 1966), p. 710.

18. Robert W. Tucker, *The Just War: A Study in Contemporary American Doctrine* (Baltimore: Johns Hopkins Press, 1960), p. 19. For a discussion of the various nuances in different usages of the term "military necessity," see W. G. Downey, Jr., "The Law of War and Military Necessity," *American Journal of International Law* 47 (April 1953): 251-54.

19. Richard A. Falk, "The Legal Control of Force in the International Community," in *The Strategy of World Order*, ed. Richard A. Falk and Saul H. Mendlovitz (New York: World Law Fund, 1966), p. 317. Of course, the concepts *raison d'etat* and *bellum iustum* both have long histories. The theoretical origins of "reason of state" can be found in Giovanni Botero's sixteenth-century book *Della ragione di stato*, while references to "just war" date back to the works of St. Ambrose in the fourth century. But as stated earlier, our focus will be upon fluctuations in the importance attached to these concepts following the Congress of Vienna.

20. Morton A. Kaplan and Nicholas deB. Katzenbach, *The Political Foundations of International Law* (New York: John Wiley & Sons, 1961), p. 206.

21. Kelsen, for instance, contends that Article 231 of the Versailles Treaty presupposes the just war doctrine:

This article justifies the reparation imposed on Germany by maintaining that Germany and her allies were responsible for an act of aggression. This means that Article 231 characterizes this aggression as an illegal act, as a delict. The article does not refer to the violation by Germany and her allies of particular treaties prohibiting war, such as the treaties guaranteeing the neutrality of Belgium and

Luxembourg. The delict for which Germany and her allies are made responsible is "aggression" in general, that is, resort to war in violation of general international law, which would be impossible if the authors of the peace treaty had shared the opinion that every state had a right to resort to war for any reason against any other state.

Hans Kelsen, *Principles of International Law* 2nd ed. (New York: Holt, Rinehart, and Winston, 1967), pp. 33-34.

22. Hans J. Morgenthau, *Politics Among Nations, The Struggle for Power and Peace* 3rd. ed. (New York: Alfred A. Knopf, 1966), p. 241. Also, Karl Ernst Jeismann, *Das Problem des Präventivkrieges im europäischen Staatensystem, mit besonderem Blick auf die Bismarckzeit* (Frieberg: Karl Alber, 1957).

23. See Edvard Kardelj, *Socialism and War* (London: Methven, 1960).

24. Richard W. Sterling, *Macropolitics, International Relations in a Global Society* (New York: Alfred A. Knopf, 1974), pp. 277-78.

25. Charles W. Fenwick, *International Law* 3rd ed. (New York: Appleton-Century-Crofts, 1948), p. 612.

26. William L. Tung, *International Law in an Organizing World* (New York: Thomas Y. Crowell, 1968), p. 461. Emphasis added.

27. Charles De Visscher, *Theory and Reality in Public International Law*, trans. P. E. Corbett, rev. ed. (Princeton: Princeton University Press, 1968), p. 49.

28. See F. Déak, "Neutrality Revisited," in *Transnational Law in a Changing Society*, ed. Wolfgang Friedmann, Louis Henkin, and Oliver J. Lissitzyn (New York: Columbia University Press, 1972), p. 154; or Gerhard von Glahn, *Law Among Nations* (New York: Macmillan, 1965), p. 630.

29. For example, Richard N. Swift, *International Law: Current and Classic* (New York: John Wiley & Sons, 1969), p. 516; and Urban G. Whitaker, Jr., *Politics and Power, A Text in International Law* (New York: Harper & Row, 1964), p. 533.

30. See J. Belin, *La Suisse et les Nations Unies* (New York: Manhattan Publishing Company, 1956), pp. 80-81. It should be added, however, that the conceptualization of just war found in the works of Bynkershoek and Pufendorf are major exceptions to this assertion. Both writers sought to limit interstate violence by acknowledging that belligerents should possess a just cause, yet they also warned neutrals against entering any ongoing disputes regardless of the merits of either belligerent's position.

31. Fenwick, *International Law*, pp. 617-18.

32. L. Oppenheim, *International Law, A Treatise*, ed. H. Lauterpacht, Vol. II, 7th ed. (New York: David MacKay, 1952), pp. 460-61.

33. De Visscher, *Theory and Reality*, p. 49.

34. Stanley Hoffmann, "International Systems and International Law," in *The International System: Theoretical Essays*, ed. Klaus Knorr and Sidney Verba (Princeton: Princeton University Press, 1961), p. 220.

35. Percey E. Corbett, *Law and Society in the Relations of States* (New York: Harcourt, Brace and Company, 1951), p. 224.

36. Hermann Kantorowicz, *The Definition of Law*, ed. A. H. Campbell (Cambridge: Cambridge University Press, 1958), p. 1.

37. Laura Nader, "The Anthropological Study of Law," *American Anthropologist* 67 (December 1965): 6.

38. For Mr. Justice Gray's classic statement on this matter see *The Paquete Habana Case*, 175 U.S. 677 (1900). Article 38 of the Statute of the International Court of Justice also recognizes the "teachings of the most highly qualified publicists of the various nations, as subsidiary means for the determination of rules of law."

39. Ole R. Holsti, *Content Analysis for the Social Sciences and Humanities* (Reading, Mass.: Addison-Wesley Publishing Company, 1969), p. 1n. See also Fred N. Kerlinger, *Foundations of Behavioral Research* (New York: Holt, Rinehart and Winston, 1964), p. 539.

40. Robert C. North, Ole R. Holsti, M. George Zaninovich, and Dina A. Zinnes, *Content Analysis* (Evanston, Ill.: Northwestern University Press, 1963), p. 51.

41. The operational procedures used to convert the information found in legal texts into machine-readable data are outlined in Charles W. Kegley, Jr., Kyungsook Choi, and Gregory A. Raymond, "Coder's Manual for the Transnational Rules Indicators Project (TRIP)," mimeographed, Institute of International Studies, University of South Carolina, 1974. A discussion of these data can be found in Charles W. Kegley, Jr., "Measuring the Growth and Decay of Transnational Norms Relevant to the Control of Violence: A Prospectus for Research," *Denver Journal of International Law and Policy* 5 (Fall 1975): 425–39; and Gregory A. Raymond, "The Transnational Rules Indicator Project: An Interim Report," *International Studies Notes* 4 (spring 1977): 12–16.

CHAPTER 3

Identifying the Structural Correlates of Arbitral Activity

There is an immense variety of empirical modes of conflict regulation. . . . Conciliation, mediation, and arbitration, and their normative and structural prerequisites, are the outstanding mechanisms for reducing . . . conflict.

— *Ralf Dahrendorf*

An Approach to Conceptualizing the Structural Attributes of the International System

The preceding chapter argues that legal norms shape the actions that take place within the international system by communicating to national actors a set of symbols expressing prevailing attitudes about specific types of behavior. At the same time that the actors are being affected by the cultural attributes of the international system they are being affected by the system's structural attributes. This chapter will focus on three concepts which reflect the structural attributes of the international system: capability distribution, status hierarchy, and intergovernmental bonds.

The reason for selecting these three concepts is quite simple. Previous research has shown that differential changes in capability tend to intensify international violence by increasing the level of status inconsistency within the state system. Not only does status inconsistency appear to have a direct impact upon war, but furthermore, it seems to actuate conflict in at least two indirect ways. On the one hand, by reducing the growth of international organization membership, it removes a key restraint upon upward spiraling arms races. On the other hand, it stimulates alliance aggregation, increasing the likelihood of open belligerency through rising armed forces levels.[1] Although these findings are tentative, they nonetheless suggest that the interrelationship among capability distribution, status hierarchy, and intergovernmental bonds is pivotal for understanding conflict behavior. Might not these same theoretical concepts also hold great potential for explaining arbitral activity? On the assumption that this is the case, the following propositions were abstracted from the literature on the structural attributes of the international system.

System Structure and Arbitral Activity

Except for propositions 13.1 and 13.2, all of the propositions covered thus far have been of the first order; that is to say, they have described trends and periodicities in the incidence of some variable over time. Since this kind of existential knowledge already exists with regard to capability distribution, status hierarchy, and intergovernmental bonds, this chapter will only examine those second-order propositions which tie these concepts to arbitration.

Proposition 14.1: There is a direct relationship between the degree of capability concentration among major powers and the amount of arbitral activity within the international system.

Proposition 14.2: There is an inverse relationship between the degree of capability concentration among major powers and the amount of arbitral activity within the international system. One of the most important issues presently facing the world community is whether the diffusion of military and economic power can be organized in ways that lead to peace rather than war. Although considered a current problem, similar questions have been debated since the fifth century. Augustine and Dante, for instance, both felt that peace was possible only in a unipolar system, while later writers such as Cruce, Rousseau, and the duc de Sully believed that the best guarantee against war was preventing the emergence of a hegemonic state.[2] Just as classical philosophers were divided over the impact of polarity upon state behavior, so too contemporary theorists disagree about the international ramifications of capability concentration. But unlike earlier debates the argument now pertains to consequences of the distribution of power among major actors rather than the efficacy of a unipolar system.[3]

One school of thought on this parity-preponderance dispute maintains that the probability of war decreases whenever military power is concentrated in the hands of a few countries.[4] While a consensus has yet to materialize over the precise threshold deemed necessary,[5] most scholars of this persuasion state that high levels of capability concentration breed order and predictability since mutual spheres of interest are clearly defined, and the dominant actors are able to moderate the use of force by others.[6] Given this premise, amicable procedures of grievance settlement presumably would flourish within such an environment.

In opposition to this view, many individuals contend that a relatively equal distribution of capabilities "is the only alternative to international anarchy on the one hand, or to a Roman solution to the problem of international peace on the other."[7] Various reasons are given for this assertion. Following the logic of Deutsch and Singer,[8] some observers suggest that parity configurations offer greater interaction opportunities for major powers and therefore decrease the attention allocated to conflict with any particular actor. By way of contrast, other authors see a parallel between the international political system and national economic systems. Modelski declares that markets dominated by a few large firms are subject to the instabilities of cutthroat competition, and the "havoc that is liable to be wrought by the collapse of one of these giants."[9] Thus instead of being conducive to peaceful intercourse, situations of preponderance are seen by this group as inherently unstable.

Empirical studies to date have merely begun spadework on this debate. Nevertheless, three clues regarding the possible impact of capability concentration on system behavior have been turned up by these efforts. First, Singer, Bremer, and Stuckey report a positive relationship between capability concentration and the magnitude of major power interstate war underway in the nineteenth century, but negative correlations for the twentieth century and the entire 1820–1965 time span.[10] Second, Haas discloses that increases in polarity are directly related to the frequency of war, the number of states at war, and deaths per war.[11] Finally, Haas has also uncovered a negative correlation between multipolarity and the use of legal means to change rules governing diplomatic relations.[12] In the light of this evidence, it seems plausible to hypothesize that increases in capability concentration are associated with a rise in the resort to pacific modes of redress.

Proposition 15.1: There is a direct relationship between the degree of capability movement among major powers and the amount of arbitral activity within the international system.

Proposition 15.2: There is an inverse relationship between the degree of capability movement among major powers and the amount of arbitral activity within the international system. An important corollary to the parity model discussed above states that the amount of international violence is determined by the rate at which capabilities move between major powers. The rationale behind this assertion lies in the alleged impact of uncertainty upon behavior. Since relative strength is difficult to assess during periods of fluidity, national leaders are said to be wary of engaging potential adversaries on the battlefield whenever capabilities are in a state of flux. Shifts in the distribution of power, therefore, may prompt states to use peaceful means to settle disputes.[13]

Advocates of the preponderance model disagree. In their estimation any such flexibility would impede conflict management. They insist that if we are to curtail the incidence of warfare, obstacles to decision-maker misperception must be eradicated. Thus as long as the apportionment of capabilities between major powers remains fixed and conspicuous, the possibility of war through miscalculation will be minimized.

On what grounds are we to choose between these competing perspectives? The evidence from relevant data-based research provides some support for each model. Increases in the amount of capability movement have been found to covary directly with the magnitude of major power interstate war underway,[14] but tight polarization has been associated with: decreasing regulatory capacity; a lack of cross-pole cooperation; the displacement of pragmatic considerations by ideological calculations; a decline in the utilization of legal procedures to change rules governing state relations; and an emphasis upon procedurality in juridical matters rather than resolving substantive issues.[15] In view of these latter findings, it appears reasonable to expect a positive relationship to obtain between capability movement and the scope, amplitude, and intensity of arbitral activity.

Proposition 16: There is an inverse relationship between the degree of status inconsistency within the international system and the amount of arbitral activity. Thus far we have been engaged in horizontal analysis. By canvassing academic opinion about the implications of major power capability distribution, our attention has been restricted to one stratum in the world community. Obviously, it is also possible to look at system structure from a vertical standpoint. As even a cursory review of sociological literature will show, knowledge of hierarchical position and perceived differences in separate rank dimensions is critical for understanding interpersonal behavior. Given the popularity of this theoretical approach on the national level, it is not surprising that the number of applications to global society has begun to grow.[16]

Those who concentrate on international stratification usually trace the roots of war to status inconsistency, that is to discrepancies between a country's achieved and ascribed status. Interestingly, many of the same assumptions which underlie this view are implicit in more conventional discussions of the international pecking order. For example, friction between satisfied and unsatisfied states has long been considered a potential source of violence,[17] and law has been traditionally acknowledged as a bulwark of the *status quo* invoked primarily by the satiated.[18] Moreover, provided that the malcontent lacks the capability to change the prevailing social order, it customarily has been granted that mutual roles would be clearly defined, and thus peace would reign. In short, the outbreak of war has been pictured as imminent whenever powerful but dissatisfied states sought a degree of prestige comparable with their achieved status.

To what extent has current empirical research on status inconsistency supported this thesis? System level studies by both East[19] and Wallace[20] have concluded that increases in the amount of systemic status inconsistency are associated with a rise in international violence. Since this pattern holds consistently despite considerable differences in the temporal domain and operational indicators employed, we may anticipate that the use of amicable modes of redress within the system will be inversely related to the degree of status inconsistency.

Proposition 17: There is an inverse relationship between the degree of status mobility within the international system and the amount of arbitral activity. A second aspect of international stratification which has received serious attention is the degree of movement within the global status hierarchy. Although upward mobility may result in greater support for the legal system in the long run,[21] most theorists presume that status movement bears the potential for conflict because: a nation undergoing a loss of status may resort to violence in an effort to salvage its prestige; top powers may launch a preventive war to maintain their privileged position; or an ascendant state may undertake offensive military action due to a miscalculation of its new but untested strength. Whether war actually occurs, we are told, depends upon the rate of status mobility.[22] As Steiner has expressed it: "Periods of rapid societal evolution are generally periods of relative lawlessness and anarchy."[23] While such reasoning suggests that status mobility and arbitral activity are inversely related, a recent study by East casts some doubt on this hypothesis. In his analysis of 115 countries between 1950 and 1964, highly mobile states were found not to be excessively conflictual.[24] Despite this evidence, a negative correlation can be expected since East's study was done on the state level and much of the theoretical literature on this matter indicates that the relationship exists primarily on the systemic level.

Proposition 18.1: There is a direct relationship between the degree of alliance aggregation within the international system and the amount of arbitral activity.

Proposition 18.2: There is an inverse relationship between the degree of alliance aggregation within the international system and the amount of arbitral activity. Besides dissecting world society horizontally and vertically, one may also make a diagonal cut across the system's structure; in other words, it is possible to delve into the distribution of power among the most prominent states, the degree of stratification throughout the globe, and the linkages between nodes of capability concentration on the major power plateau and actors on each of the strata below. Alliance networks comprise one of the most prominent intergovernmental bonds within this latter category. But irrespective of their import and the close scrutiny they have received, theorists diverge markedly over their impact on the international system. It has variously been asserted that alliances "neither limit nor expand conflicts any more than they cause or prevent them;"[25] that they stabilize the system;[26] and that they "give additional momentum to the anarchic forces in international society."[27] Consequently, no consensus has emerged on whether alliances provide a foundation for further regional and world cooperation. As Friedman summarizes the current outlook, an alliance "strengthens international law to the extent that it contributes to the structuring of the community of nations."[28] Nevertheless, "international law is also threatened by the excessive aggregation of power that alliance can produce."[29]

What light has scientific research shed on this question? Singer and Small report that a relationship exists between the level of commitments in the system and the outbreak of war, but add that the direction of the relationship depends upon the period being analyzed: during the nineteenth century a negative association existed between alliance aggregation and the onset of war, whereas in the twentieth century a positive association appeared.[30] However, when the data were not divided by diplomatic era, a positive relationship materialized.[31] Since some question remains over the breakpoints used in the first study reported, and since increases in alliance aggregation have been connected with upward surges in the amount of war begun throughout the 1815–1965 time span, it is anticipated that they will furthermore be associated with reduction in the use of pacific modes of dispute settlement.

Proposition 19: There is a direct relationship between the amount of international organization within the international system and the amount of arbitral activity. Like alliances, international organizations are a bond whose origins extend into antiquity. Athough some have denied their capacity to resolve conflicts,[32] many contemporary writers continue to outline their merits in much the same way as had Dubois, Kant, and the Abbé de Saint-Pierre. The rationale for this unflagging endorsement can be found in the assertion that international organizations provide a consensual foundation for the state system. That is to say, they "play a leading and indispensable role" in fostering conceptions of duty, obligation, and the rule of law;[33] and therefore have made "notable gains in the field of noncoercive regulatory devices."[34] One such gain, it is argued, lies in the impetus they have given to arbitral activity.[35] But the evidence supporting this position is slim. Recent quantitative research has shown that international organizations have only negligible impact upon the amount of war which occurs in the system.[36] While this finding does not disprove the hypothesized direct relationship between international organizations and the incidence of arbitration, it does erode an initial premise upon which the proposition rests.

Now that a propositional inventory has been put together on the structural correlates of arbitral activity, the testing process may begin. Table 3.1 describes the variables that were used to operationalize the concepts of capability distribution, status hierarchy, and intergovernmental bonds. Data on these variables were aggregated for each half- decade within the 1820–1964 time span and then normalized for system size.[37] In the analysis which follows, lagged delta values $(x_t - x_{t-1})$ of these variables were correlated with delta values of the scope, amplitude, and intensity of arbitral activity.[38]

Table 3.2 gives the analysis results for the two variables which pertain to capability distribution. As anticipated, a positive association was found between capability concentration and each dimension of arbitral activity. Although this finding supports proposition 14.1, the support is not overwhelming since the relationship between capability concentration and scope is quite weak. Likewise, the correlations between capability movement and arbitral activity are also weak. Contrary to our original expectations, two of the three relationships are inverse. In the light of this occurrence, proposition 15.2 appears to describe best the impact of shifts in the distribution of power upon international arbitration.

A look at Table 3.3 shows that the hypotheses drawn from the concept of status hierarchy fare no better than those derived from the theoretical literature on capability distribution. The predicted negative correlation between status inconsistency and arbitral activity only appears in the intensity dimension. Secondly, although all of the correlations involving status mobility conform to the direction anticipated, none are strong enough to give us much

Table 3.1 A List of the Structural Attributes under Investigation

Concept	Variable	Indicator	Abbreviation	Data Source
Capability distribution	Major power capability concentration	The extent to which demographic, industrial, and military capabilities are concentrated among nations in the major power subsystem.	CON	J. David Singer, Stuart Bremer, and John Stuckey, "Capability Distribution, Uncertainty, and Major Power War, 1820—1965," in *Peace, War, and Numbers,* ed. by Bruce M. Russett (Beverly Hills, Calif.: Sage Publications, 1972), pp. 19—48.
	Major power capability movement	The number of percentage of capability shares which have been exchanged within the major power subsystem.	MOVE	J. David Singer, Stuart Bremer, and John Stuckey, "Capability Distribution, Uncertainty, and Major Power War, 1820—1965," in *Peace, War, and Numbers,* ed. by Bruce M. Russett (Beverly Hills, Calif.: Sage Publications, 1972), pp. 19—48.
Status hierarchy	Status inconsistency	The sum of the differences between the rank position of each nation on the status dimensions of military personnel and diplomatic importance.	STATIN	Michael D. Wallace, *War and Rank Among Nations* (Lexington, Mass.: D.C. Heath & Company, 1973).
	Status mobility	The standard deviation of the national rates of change on the status dimension of diplomatic importance.	STATMOB	Michael D. Wallace, *War and Rank Among Nations* (Lexington, Mass.: D.C. Heath & Company, 1973).
Intergovernmental bonds	Alliance aggregation	The percentage of nations having at least one alliance of any type with any other nation.	ALAG	J. David Singer and Melvin Small, "Formal Alliances, 1815—1939: A Quantitative Description," *Journal of Peace Research* 3 (1966): 1—32; and Melvin Small and J. David Singer, "Formal Alliances, 1816—1945: An Extension of the Basic Data," *Journal of Peace Research* 6 (1969): 257—82.
	Amount of international organization	The number of nation-memberships in organizations, weighted by diplomatic importance.	IGO	Michael D. Wallace and J. David Singer, "International Organization in the Global System, 1815—1964: A Quantitative Description," *International Organization* 29 (Spring 1970): 239—87.

Table 3.2   The Impact of Capability Distribution upon International Arbitration

Dimension of Arbitral Activity	Correlation with Capability Concentration			
	b	r	r^2	$\hat{s_y}$
Scope	.23	.07	.00	.22
Amplitude	1.88	.57	.34	.17
Intensity	.25	.47	.22	.03

Dimension of Arbitral Activity	Correlation with Capability Movement			
	b	r	r^2	$\hat{s_y}$
Scope	.51	.13	.02	.22
Amplitude	−.42	−.12	.01	.21
Intensity	−.15	−.26	.07	.03

Table 3.3   The Impact of Status Hierarchy upon International Arbitration

Dimension of Arbitral Activity	Correlation with Status Inconsistency			
	b	r	r^2	$\hat{s_y}$
Scope	1.26	.22	.05	.21
Amplitude	.98	.18	.03	.20
Intensity	−1.15	−.17	.03	.03

Dimension of Arbitral Activity	Correlation with Status Mobility			
	b	r	r^2	$\hat{s_y}$
Scope	−.01	−.01	.00	.22
Amplitude	−.05	−.07	.01	.21
Intensity	−.01	−.01	.00	.04

confidence in this outcome. Consequently, neither proposition 16 nor proposition 17 can be maintained in the face of the empirical evidence.

Turning last to the impact of intergovernmental bonds upon arbitration, Table 3.4 shows that once again the results do not give much support to our earlier speculations. When alliance aggregation is correlated with the intensity, the direct relationship predicted by proposition 18.1 appears.

However, the implications flowing from the analysis of the remaining two dimensions of arbitral activity are less clear. On one hand, the correlation with amplitude is positive in direction but negligible in size, on the other hand, the correlation with scope is slightly larger, but points in the opposite direction. Similar results show up in those correlations involving international organization. If one examines only the dimension of intensity, then proposition 19 seems reasonable. But inspection of scope and amplitude lead to the conclusion that a positive relationship between changes in the amount of international organization within the system and changes in the level of arbitral activity does not exist.

Table 3.4   The Impact of Intergovernmental Bonds upon International Arbitration

Dimension of Arbitral Activity	Correlation with Alliance Aggregation			
	b	r	r^2	$s\hat{y}$
Scope	−.17	−.10	.01	.22
Amplitude	.05	.03	.00	.21
Intensity	.06	.24	.06	.01

Dimension of Arbitral Activity	Correlation with International Organization			
	b	r	r^2	$s\hat{y}$
Scope	−.01	−.02	.00	.23
Amplitude	.01	.03	.00	.21
Intensity	.01	.20	.04	.03

What conclusions can one draw about the structural correlates of arbitral activity on the basis of the preceding analysis? It may seem as if we have performed a wrecking operation. Indeed, it might even appear that there is little that can be salvaged from the heap of unsubstantiated propositions behind us. Nevertheless, three important results have been obtained. First, insofar as the coefficients of determination were negligible for all of the relationships involving certain variables (e.g., STATMOB), we can eliminate them from further consideration as potential sources of arbitral activity. Second, because many of the variables appear to exert a differential impact upon each dimension of arbitral activity, we can assume that the causal connections between structural attributes and arbitration are more complex than initially imagined. Finally, since some of the variables did survive this bivariate analysis, we shall be able to incorporate them within a larger multivariable model of the determinants of arbitral activity. In summary, we may conclude this chapter much the same way we concluded Chapter 2, that is with an acknowledgment that any full presentation of those conditions which lead to increases in arbitration will necessarily include variables from both the cultural and structural attributes of the international system. Of course, this raises some important questions. How do these variables all fit together in a multicausal explanation of international arbitration? Which variables are the most potent in accounting for the scope, amplitude, and intensity of arbitral activity? It is to these questions that we shall now turn.

Notes

1. Michael D. Wallace, "Status, Formal Organization, and Arms Levels as Factors Leading to the Onset of War, 1820-1964," in *Peace, War, and Numbers*, ed. Bruce M. Russett (Beverly Hills, Calif.: Sage Publications, 1972), pp. 62-66.

2. See August C. Krey, "The International State of the Middle Ages: Some Reasons for Its Failure," *American Historical Review* 28 (October 1922): 1-12; and Karl W. Deutch, "Changing Images of International Conflict," *Journal of Social Issues* 23 (January 1967): 91-95. The term polarity is used here to describe the degree of capability concentration observable at a particular point in time. Modelski distinguishes between this concept and polarization, i.e. the process by which other states come to revolve around one or more of these poles. George Modelski, *World Power Concentration: Typology, Data, Explanatory Framework* (Morristown, N.J.: General Learning Press, 1974), p. 4.

3. A notable exception is George Liska, *Imperial America: The International Politics of Primacy* (Baltimore: Johns Hopkins Press, 1967).

4. Examples of this position include: Raymond Aron, "The Quest for a Philosophy of Foreign Affairs," in *Contemporary Theory in International Relations*, ed. Stanley Hoffmann (Englewood Cliffs, N.J.: Prentice-Hall, 1960), pp. 79-91; Raymond F. Hopkins and Richard W. Mansbach,

Structure and Process in International Politics (New York: Harper & Row, 1973), pp. 110–12; Charles P. Schleicher, *International Relations, Cooperation and Conflict* (Englewood Cliffs, N.J.: Prentice-Hall, 1962), p. 138; John G. Stoessinger, *The Might of Nations* (New York: Random House, 1961), p. 180; and Robert Strauz-Hupé and Stefan Possony, *International Relations in the Age of Conflict Between Democracy and Dictatorship* (New York: McGraw-Hill, 1950).

5. See Kenneth N. Waltz, "The Stability of a Bipolar World," *Daedalus* 93 (summer 1964): 881–907; and George W. Ball, *The Discipline of Power* (Boston: Little, Brown & Company, 1967), p. 349.

6. For an elaboration of this position, see Kenneth N. Waltz, "International Structure, National Force, and the Balance of World Power," *Journal of International Affairs* 21 (1967): 229.

7. Eugene V. Rostow, *Peace in the Balance* (New York: Simon and Schuster, 1972), p. 323. Also see his *Law, Power, and the Pursuit of Peace* (Lincoln, Neb.: University of Nebraska Press, 1968), p. 22.

8. Karl W. Deutsch and J. David Singer, "Multipolar Power Systems and International Stability," *World Politics* 16 (April 1964): 390–406.

9. George Modelski, *Principles of World Politics* (New York: Free Press, 1972), p. 137.

10. J. David Singer, Stuart Bremer, and John Stuckey, "Capability Distribution, Uncertainty, and Major Power War, 1820–1965," in Russett, ed., *Peace, War, and Numbers*, p. 33.

11. Michael Haas, "International Subsystems: Stability and Polarity," *American Political Science Review* 64 (March 1970): 98–121.

12. Michael Haas, *International Conflict* (Indianapolis, Ind.: Bobbs-Merrill Company, 1974), p. 406.

13. Frederick H. Hartmann, *The Relations of Nations* 4th ed. (New York: Macmillan, 1973), pp. 361–62, 630; and Ernst B. Haas and Allen S. Whiting, *Dynamics of International Relations* (New York: McGraw-Hill, 1956), p. 50.

14. Singer et al., "Capability Distribution," pp. 33–42. Although an inverse relationship was found during the nineteenth century, the bivariate coefficient of determination was very small, as were the squared partial correlation coefficients in each of the four versions of the multivariate equations.

15. Haas, *International Conflict*, pp. 401–417.

16. The initial efforts in this direction may be seen in Gustavo Lagos, *International Stratification and Underdeveloped Countries* (Chapel Hill, N.C.: University of North Carolina Press, 1963); and in the following works by Johan Galtung: "A Structural Theory of Aggression," *Journal of Peace Research* 1 (1964): 95–119; "Rank and Social Integration: A Multidimensional Approach," in *Sociological Theories in Progress*, Vol. I, ed. Joseph Berger, Morris Zelditch, Jr. and Bo Anderson (Boston: Houghton Mifflin, 1966), pp. 145–98; and "International Relations and International Conflicts: A Sociological Approach," *Transactions of the Sixth World Congress of Sociology* 1 (September 1966): 121–61.

17. See Frederick L. Schuman, *International Politics, Anarchy and*

Order in the World Society 7th ed. (New York: McGraw-Hill, 1969), pp. 274-76.

18. See Hans J. Morgenthau, *Politics Among Nations, The Struggle for Power and Peace* 3rd ed. (New York: Alfred A. Knopf, 1966), p. 427; and Vernon Van Dyke, *International Politics* 2nd ed. (New York: Appleton-Century-Crofts, 1966), pp. 270-71.

19. Maurice A. East, "Status Discrepancy and Violence in the International System: An Empirical Analysis," in *The Analysis of International Politics*, ed. James N. Rosenau, Vincent Davis, and Maurice A. East (New York: Free Press, 1972), pp. 299-319.

20. Michael D. Wallace, "Power, Status and International War," *Journal of Peace Research*, 1 (1971): 23-35.

21. Less-developed states, it is argued, represent a challenge to the prevailing normative structure of the international system. But as their capabilities and status rise, their attitude toward international law allegedly begins to change. See Cecil V. Crabb, Jr., *Nations in a Multipolar World* (New York: Harper & Row, 1968), pp. 137-40; and Wolfgang Friedman, *The Changing Structure of International Law* (New York: Columbia University Press, 1964), p. 318.

22. A. F. K. Organski, *World Politics* (New York: Alfred A. Knopf, 1958), pp. 334-35, 440.

23. H. Arthur Steiner, *Principles and Problems of International Relations* (New York: Harper & Brothers, 1940), p. 208.

24. Maurice A. East, "Rank-Dependent Interaction and Mobility: Two Aspects of International Stratification," *Peace Research Society Papers* 14 (1969): 127.

25. George Liska, *Nations in Alliance: The Limits of Interdependence* (Baltimore: Johns Hopins Press, 1962), p. 138.

26. Charles O. Lerche, Jr. and Abdul A. Said, *Concepts in International Politics* (Englewood Cliffs, N.J.: Prentice-Hall, Inc., 1963), p. 116.

27. Georg Schwarzenberger, *Power Politics* 3rd ed. (New York: Frederick A. Praeger, 1964), p. 167.

28. Julian R. Friedman, "Alliance in International Politics," in *Alliance in International Politics*, ed. Julian R. Friedman, Christopher Bladen, and Steven Rosen (Boston: Allyn and Bacon, 1970), p. 28.

29. Ibid., p. 29.

30. J. David Singer and Melvin Small, "Alliance Aggregation and the Onset of War, 1815-1945," in *Quantitative International Politics: Insights and Evidence*, ed. J. David Singer (New York: Free Press, 1968), p. 282.

31. See J. David Singer and Melvin Small, "National Alliance Commitments and War Involvement, 1815-1945," *Peace Research Society Papers* 5 (1966): 109-40. For a recent qualification in regard to major powers, see. J. David Singer and Melvin Small, "War in History and in the State of the World Message," in *Analyzing International Relations: A Multimethod Introduction*, ed. William D. Coplin and Charles W. Kegley, Jr. (New York: Praeger Publishers, 1975), pp. 236-37.

32. See Charles V. Reynolds, *Theory and Explanation in International Politics* (New York: Barnes and Noble, 1973), p. 274. A more balanced

assessment is given in Charles Easton Rothwell, "International Organization and World Politics," in Goodrich and Kay, *International Organization*, p. 33; and Harold Sprout and Margaret Sprout, *Foundations of International Politics* (Princeton: D. Van Nostrand Company, Inc., 1962), p. 570.

33. E. F. Penrose, *The Revolution in International Relations* (London: Frank Cass & Co., 1965), p. 278. See also Leo Gross, "The Development of International Law through the United Nations," in *The United Nations: Past, Present, and Future*, ed. James Barros (New York: Free Press, 1972), pp. 171-217.

34. Inis L. Claude, *Swords into Plowshares, The Problems and Progress of International Organization*, 3rd ed., revised (New York: Random House, 1964), p. 394.

35. This point has been made particularly in regard to the League of Nations. See Gerhard von Glahn, *Law Among Nations*, 2nd ed. (New York: Macmillan, 1970), p. 467.

36. On the contrary, the amount of war ending influences international organization growth during the next decade. Moreover, increases in the severity of war are associated with a rise in the number and size of international organizations. See respectively J. David Singer and Michael Wallace, "Intergovernmental Organization and the Preservation of Peace, 1816-1964: Some Bivariate Relationships," *International Organization* 24 (summer 1970): 520-47; and Kjell Skjelsback, "Shared Memberships in Intergovernmental Organizations and Dyadic War, 1864-1964," in *The United Nations: Problems and Prospects*, ed. Edwin Fedder (St. Louis, Mo.: Center for International Studies, 1971), pp. 31-62.

37. At this point, a methodological note is in order. The temporal domain selected for study covers the period from 1815 through 1969. In certain instances, however, a slightly smaller domain was employed because some of the structural attribute data did not begin until 1820 and ended in 1964. Aside from this, two other nuances in the data should be noted. First, the values of STATIN begin five years later than the values of the other variables, while STATMOB ends a half-decade sooner. Second, the observational periods for CON, MOVE, STATIN, and STATMOB have been altered during World Wars I and II in order to minimize any distortions these periods would give to those indicators based upon national capabilities.

38. Prior to the correlation and regression analysis, the data were tested for trend and serial correlation. The results indicated that when delta values were used neither of the above factors would seriously contaminate the study. In addition, visual inspection of the bivariate scatterplots for each hypothesized relationship suggested that curvilinear models would not fit the data any better than a simple linear model.

CHAPTER 4

The Relative Potency of Legal Norms and System Structure in Inductive-Statistical Explanations of Arbitral Activity

The careful reworking of verbal theories is undoubtedly one of the most challenging tasks confronting us. The major portion of this enterprise will undoubtedly consist of clarifying concepts, eliminating or consolidating variables, . . . searching the literature for propositions, and looking for implicit assumptions connecting the major propositions in important theoretical works. The final translation into formal mathematics . . . would seem to be a relatively simpler task.
—Hubert M. Blalock, Jr.

From Correlational to Explanatory Knowledge

Up to this point, two steps have been taken in the quest for an empirical theory of international arbitration. In the first chapter existential knowledge about changes in the scope, amplitude, and intensity of arbitral activity over the past century and a half was established. In the next two chapters, correlational knowledge was obtained about the relationship between these changes and prior changes in the cultural and structural attributes of the international system. Having thus acquired two basic kinds of knowledge about international arbitration, we shall now seek a third kind of knowledge: how legal norms and system structure fit together in a multicausal explanation of arbitral activity.

If we are ever to know the causes of international arbitration, we must from the outset be clear on what counts as an explanation. Unfortunately, although explanatory knowledge is widely accepted as the ultimate aim of scientific inquiry, there is considerable disagreement among researchers over the question: What is it for something to be explained in social science? The term "explanation" will be understood here as referring to nomological accounts of a given phenomenon. Roughly speaking, nomological explanations enable us to understand why a phenomenon occurred by showing that it was a particular instance of a general pattern. This is accomplished when two types of sentences are connected: those which describe the so-called facts of the situation on hand, and those which link specific causes to specific effects without regard to any spatiotemporal domain. Thus a nomological explanation for a given phenomenon y_i would entail: (1) establishing that condition x_i existed in the situation under investigation; (2) demonstrating that x_i was a particular instance of X; (3) knowing the general pattern that prior instances of X cause instances of Y to occur at a subsequent point in time; and (4) demonstrating that y_i was a particular instance of Y.[1]

The heart of a nomological explanation is the theoretical statement which links cause with effect. Whenever this statement is a universal generalization (if X, then always Y), the explanation may be conceived as a deductive argument whose conclusions logically follow from the premises. Deductive nomological explanations abound in the physical sciences but, as one writer has put it, they have become an albatross around the neck of the social sciences.[2] Quite simply, the social sciences cannot meet the most fundamental requirement for deductive explanation. Instead of possessing universal generalizations that hold without exception, the explanans of most social scientific explanations contain contingency generalizations (if X, then probably Y) which only confer inductive support upon the explanandum.[3] Nevertheless, this does not preclude one from building an empirical theory. Probabilistic statements play important roles in many of the nomological explanations given for phenomena in such diverse fields as mechanics and genetics. Hence there is no reason to assume that contingency generalizations will be any less useful in arriving at inductive-statistical explanations of those phenomena studied by the social sciences.

Buried in this last point is the rationale behind all of the foregoing. Because the field of international relations has been sorely lacking in the universal statements required for deductive explanations, it has become rather heavily inductive. However, should empirical research establish contingency generalizations about various types of behavior within the international system, it will still be possible to arrive at nomological explanations of that behavior. Put another way, if we can build a theory out of contingency generalizations about the sources of arbitral activity, then we shall be in a position to understand what systemic conditions would produce future upswings in this mode of conflict resolution.

A Regression Model

One of the most important steps in building such a theory is to specify the relative potencies of those independent variables which affect the dependent variable(s) in question. As Rosenau has argued:

Only after the relevant variables have been identified and their relative potency assessed through quantitative analysis is it possible to fashion a coherent body of empirical theory. If these initial steps are neglected and efforts to build integrated theory undertaken directly, there are likely to be as many theories as there are theorists, and the convergence around a common set of concepts and findings, which is necessary to the evolution of a unified science, is not likely to occur.[4]

In selecting a model to assess the relative influence of cultural and structural attributes on arbitral activity, several methodological assumptions were made. First, it was assumed that scope, amplitude, and intensity constituted orthogonal dimensions of arbitral activity. This seemed to be warranted insofar as the zero-order intercorrelations and the first-order partial correlations between delta values of the three variables revealed no relationship stronger than the .22 association between amplitude and intensity. The second assumption held that it was possible to decompose the empirical world into blocs of hierarchical, unidimensional relationships, and then model these relationships with recursive equations whose parameters could be estimated through ordinary least-squares regression. Third, it was further assumed that the dynamic nature of reality could be captured in these equations by the use of rates of change and lagged exogenous variables. Rates of change may be introduced into a regression equation in two ways. If time is interpreted as continuous, then rate of change may be expressed by the derivative of X with respect to time $(\Delta X/\Delta t)$ in a differential equation. Alternatively, if time is viewed in terms of discrete periods, then delta variables may be used in a difference equation. Because the data employed in this study are averages over half-decades rather than instantaneous readings such as a speedometer provides, it was assumed that difference equations would be appropriate for our purposes, even though time is in fact continuous.[5]

Taking all of these assumptions together, the model used here can be depicted as an elaboration of the general form:

if X, then probably Y

Given the number of independent variables that could affect arbitral activity, the above expression was reformulated to read:

$$Y = f(X_1 + X_2 + \ldots + X_n) + e$$

Or, in other words, each dimension of arbitral activity (Y) was seen as a function of the additive impact of certain cultural and structural attributes of the international system (X_1 through X_n) plus a stochastic term (e), which included any unspecified variables affecting Y as well as any random measurement errors. To make this mathematical relationship more precise, it was subsequently transformed into the following equation:

$$\triangle Y_t = \beta_0 + \beta_1 (\triangle X_1)_{t-1} + \beta_2 (\triangle X_2)_{t-1} + \ldots + \beta_n (\triangle X_n)_{t-1} + e$$

Finally, the model was completed by taking those variables from the two previous chapters which showed evidence of having some relationship with arbitral activity (see Table 4.1) and placing them in the equation.[6]

Table 4.1   Hypothesized Determinants of Arbitral Activity

Dimension of Arbitral Activity	Systemic Attributes Selected for Inclusion			
	Cultural	Structural		
	Pacific Settlement Norms	Capability Distribution	Status Hierarchy	Inter-governmental Bonds
Scope	SAL	MOVE	STATIN	ALAG
Amplitude	SAL	CON MOVE	STATIN	
Intensity	SAL	CON MOVE	STATIN	ALAG IGO

The statistical procedure used to assess the causal potency of these hypothesized determinants of arbitral activity was stepwise multiple regression. In essence, this technique represents "something of a halfway house between multiple regression analysis and fullblown multiequation causal models."[7] It computes a sequence of multiple linear regression equations adding that one variable at each step which makes the greatest reduction in the error sum of squares, possesses the highest correlation with the dependent variable partialed on the variables which have already been added, and has the highest F value. The use of this procedure has several advantages over standard multiple regression. Stepwise regression rank orders the independent variables according to their relative potency and, as Alker points out, this ordering has a causal interpretation in that "the various partial regression slopes measure direct effects."[8] Also, the relative potency of any independent variable calculated with standard multiple regression may be artifactual insofar as this procedure simply regresses the first predictor variable provided by the independent variable list on the dependent variable, determines the residuals, and then regresses these residuals against the second listed independent variable, and so on. Given that stepwise multiple regression iteratively searches the entire list of independent variables for the single variable which best accounts for the variance in the dependent variable and then analyzes every n-variable combination for the best model, it seems to constitute the most suitable procedure for discovering the relative potencies of the variables from Table 4.1 in an inductive-statistical explanation of arbitral activity.

Tables 4.2 through 4.4 report the results of the stepwise multiple regression analysis. Looking first at the equation which models the scope of arbitral activity, we find that perceived salience is the most potent determinant of how many states settle their disputes through international arbitration. Status inconsistency and alliance aggregation follow it in order of importance. The regression coefficients indicate that both perceived salience and status inconsistency are directly related to scope, while alliance aggregation is inversely related. In other words, the proportion of states that use arbitration tends to rise following increases in both the esteem given by the international legal culture to arbitration and the degree of rank disequilibrium within the international system. Furthermore, it tends to increase following decreases in alliance formation. Although the combination of these three variables does not account for much of the variance in scope, the multiple coefficient of determination could not be altered by adding any of our other candidate variables to the equation.

Turning next to the equation which models the amplitude of arbitral activity, we see that once again both cultural and structural attributes affect the dependent variable. But this time they account for a greater amount of the variance. The results show that capability concentration is the most potent determinant of how many major powers arbitrate their disputes. It is followed in order of importance by perceived salience, status inconsistency, and status mobility. The regression coefficients indicate that while capability concentration and status inconsistency are directly related to amplitude, salience and capability movement are inversely related. Thus when a preponderance of capabilities is concentrated in the hands of a few countries and there is little shifting in these capabilities, the proportion of major powers which use arbitration increases.

A similar conclusion may be reached when the equation which models intensity is examined. As in the previous equation, capability concentration is the most potent determinant of the dependent variable under investigation. Status inconsistency, perceived salience, and capability movement follow it in order. The signs of the regression coefficients for capability concentration and movement are the same as in the amplitude equation, however, they are reversed for status inconsistency and salience. Therefore, it may be said that states tend to arbitrate issues of great importance whenever capabilities are firmly concentrated in the hands of a few countries, a stable rank order exists among members of the international system, and arbitration is considered to be an important mode of conflict resolution.

The results indicate that the most notable instances of arbitration occur when a high, stable concentration of capabilities exists among a relatively small number of countries. Not only do major powers arbitrate their differences more often during these periods, but all states appear to arbitrate a greater proportion of important issues. Beyond

Table 4.2   A Stepwise Multiple Regression Model of the Scope of Arbitral Activity

Step Number	Variable Entered	Regression Coeffecient	Standard Error
1	SAL	.27	.19
2	STATIN	.65	1.29
3	ALAG	−.14	.37

R = .35; R^2 = .12; SEE = .22.

Table 4.3   A Stepwise Multiple Regression Model of the Amplitude of Arbitral Activity

Step Number	Variable Entered	Regression Coeffecient	Standard Error
1	CON	1.74	.58
2	SAL	−.26	.16
3	STATIN	.75	1.01
4	MOVE	−.46	.62

R = .61; R^2 = .37; SEE = .18.

Table 4.4   A Stepwise Multiple Regression Model of the Intensity of Aribitral Activity

Step Number	Variable Entered	Regression Coeffecient	Standard Error
1	CON	.28	.09
2	STATIN	−.29	.15
3	SAL	.05	.03
4	MOVE	−.16	.09

R = .68; R^2 = .46; SEE = .03

this, the data also suggest that while high levels of status discrepancy tend to be associated with greater amounts of arbitral activity, this activity generally pertains to issues which are not very important to the actors involved. Therefore, we can refine our generalization by stating that the most critical cases of arbitration occur when the following conditions are present: (1) capabilities are fixed and concentrated in the hands of a few nations; (2) a stable hierarchy of rank positions exists throughout the system; and (3) the international legal culture places a high amount of significance on conflict resolution through arbitration.

Pre-theories and the Logic of Discovery

According to Abraham Kaplan, the most basic scientific question asks "What the devil is going on around here?" Every answer to this question, he points out, is inescapably a generalization which subsumes the particularity of the goings-on under some pattern.[9] Thus in trying to be able to account for the incidence of arbitral activity at a given point in time, we have sought to discover the general pattern which has historically obtained between diachronic fluctuations in the scope, amplitude, and intensity of arbitration, and changes in specific properties of the international system. Now that this pattern has been uncovered, it remains to be seen how such a finding will add to our explanatory knowledge of international arbitration.

Perhaps the most important issue to consider in this regard centers on what we can learn from an inductive-statistical account of any phenomenon. Increasingly in recent years it has been claimed that such accounts represent some form of resurrected Baconism; that is to say they are based on an investigatory procedure which contains three main steps: (1) collection and recording of all facts; (2) the analysis and classification of these facts; and (3) an inductive derivation of generalizations from them.[10] At best, it is said that this procedure can provide us with information on the degree of association between variables; but it can never give any theoretical rationale for why that association may exist.

Even though one of the objectives of this study has been to establish the contingency generalizations needed for an inductive-statistical explanation of arbitral activity, this alone does not mean that we have engaged in the kind of barefoot empiricism described in Bacon's *Novum Organum*. To begin with, the statistical tests reported above were based upon propositions which had been derived from theoretical literature bearing arbitration. Thus the variables used in these tests, as well as their operational indicators, were selected because of their ties to the concepts in each proposition. Rather than passively accumulating all the facts "as they were" in the hope that somehow causal connections would emerge, active choices were exercised over which facts had theoretical relevance, and how these facts could be made into data. Taking all these points together, they suggest that "even the inductive political fisherman needs some theory to guide him. You have to know what pools and streams to fish in, how to select tackle, and how to manipulate the tackle."[11]

Yet, to say that the tests conducted were informed by theoretical literature is not to say that upon completion of these tests an empirical theory resulted. All in all, the literature from which those propositions were taken contained confusing and often contradictory sets of insights based on conjecture alone. What we have merely done is distinguish between those assertions which could be supported by evidence and those which could not. In essence, an empirical pre-theory has been formulated. While this enables us to generalize about the systemic determinants of arbitral activity, it does not explain why variations in these particular cultural and structural attributes account for variations in arbitral activity. Our only clues rest on the untested arguments of those theorists from whom we abstracted the propositions in the first place. A full theoretical explanation of arbitral activity would fit the contingency generalizations discovered together with other generalizations which account for changes in capability concentration, status inconsistency, capability movement, alliance aggregation, and the perceived salience of arbitration. To put the matter another way, a pre-theory is a way-station on the road to empirical theory. Although it provides evidence about the relative potencies of those independent variables which affect the dependent variable(s) in question, it lacks the same kind of evidence on what causes those independent variables to change and why these changes have the impact they do.

By way of contrast, an empirical theory links various disparate generalizations together in a novel way. Not only does it explain why the existing generalizations hold, but it also gives rise to predictions that in turn lead to new generalizations. Although no logic of discovery is known to exist, this study is grounded in a particular approach to empirical theory-building. In brief, it posits the following sequence of steps: (1) deducing propositions from theoretical literature on the subject under investigation; (2) converting these propositions into testable form; and (3) combining those variables which were distilled through statistical testing into a multivariate model. Once these steps are completed, the empirical pre-theory which results may serve as a jumping-off point for fashioning the creative ideas from which theories emerge. Consider, for instance, Kepler's theory of the elliptical orbit:

Kepler did not *begin* with the hypothesis that Mars' orbit was elliptical and then deduce statements confirmed by Brahe's observations. These latter observations were given, and they set the problem—they were Johannes Kepler's starting point. He struggled back from these, first to one hypothesis, then to another, and ultimately to the hypothesis of the elliptical orbit.[12]

To be sure, there are other approaches to theory-building. Some, like the Baconian strategy mentioned earlier, stress an inductive research-then-theory process; while others call for a more deductive theory-then-research process. Clearly the former have an inherent weakness insofar as considerable effort may be spent on collecting data that are unrelated to the problem at hand, however, the latter have the disadvantage of attempting to theorize without a bedrock of initial information. Consequently, the approach taken here is what Reynolds calls a composite of these two strategies.

Initial research is conducted in an attempt to provide suggestive patterns. . . . Once an empirical generalization is established, a theory may be constructed to explain this regularity. Resources are not wasted in gathering a lot of information expecting to find laws by searching through the data. Theories are not invented until there is some information about the phenomenon.[13]

The first aim of this study was to obtain some initial information about the extent to which changes in specific cultural and structural attributes of the international system have been associated with the use of arbitration. With this task behind us, we may extend our pre-theory. In the next chapter, we shall take up our second objective and examine the consequences of arbitral activity by analyzing the impact of arbitration on the onset of war.

Notes

1. For a more elaborate presentation, see my "Comparative Analysis and Nomological Explanation," in *International Events and the Comparative Analysis of Foreign Policy*, ed. Charles W. Kegley, Jr. et al. (Columbia, S.C.: University of South Carolina Press, 1975), pp. 41-51.

2. Eugene J. Meehan, *Explanation in Social Science: A System Paradigm* (Homewood, Ill.: Dorsey Press, 1968), p. 3.

3. Salmon contends that statistical explanations do not need to embody a high probability nor need they be interpreted as inductive inferences. Instead, he claims that it is only necessary to show that X is statistically relevant to the occurrence of Y. "To say that a certain factor is *statistically relevant* to the occurrence of an event means, roughly, that it *makes a difference to the probability of that occurrence*—that is, the probability of the event is different in the presence of that factor than in its absence." Wesley C. Salmon, *Statistical Explanation and Statistical Relevance* (Pittsburgh: University of Pittsburgh Press, 1971), p. 11.

4. James N. Rosenau, *The Scientific Study of Foreign Policy* (New York: Free Press, 1971), p. 151.

5. Carl F. Christ, *Economic Models and Methods* (New York: John Wiley & Sons, 1966), p. 177. Also see Paul A. Samuelson, *Foundations of Economic Analysis* (Cambridge: Harvard University Press, 1947), p. 315.

6. Prior to the analysis, the data were checked for multicollinearity. The delta values for the independent variables in each regression equation were not highly intercorrelated. Only three correlations were greater than .30, and none were above .40.

7. Hayward R. Alker, Jr., "Statistics and Politics: The Need for Causal

Data Analysis," in *Politics and the Social Sciences*, ed. Seymour Martin Lipset (New York: Oxford University Press, 1969), p. 256.

8. Ibid., p. 257.

9. Abraham Kaplan, *The Conduct of Inquiry* (San Francisco: Chandler Publishing Company, 1964), p. 85.

10. See Carl G. Hempel, *Philosophy of Natural Science* (Englewood Cliffs, N.J.: Prentice-Hall, 1966), p. 11.

11. Bruce M. Russett, "A Macroscopic View of International Politics," in *The Analysis of International Politics*, ed. James N. Rosenau, Vincent Davis, and Maurice A. East (New York: Free Press, 1972), p. 117.

12. N. R. Hanson, *Patterns of Discovery* (Cambridge: Cambridge University Press, 1965), p. 72.

13. Paul Davidson Reynolds, *A Primer in Theory Construction* (Indianapolis: Bobbs-Merrill, 1971), p. 156.

CHAPTER 5

International Arbitration and the Preservation of Peace

An arbitrator who agrees with (at least) one party to the dispute will be useless. But an arbitrator who agrees with no party to the dispute will also be useless. So arbitrators are not useful.

—Chuang Tzu

An Extension of the Pre-theory

When smoldering animosities between the post-Tridentine Church and advocates of religious reformation erupted into thirty years of savage conflict in 1618, the Dutch publicist Huig van Groot was moved to write that throughout the Western world he had seen a "lawlessness in warfare that even barbarian races would think shameful." Without any pretext, he observed, "Men rush to arms, and once arms are taken up, all respect for law . . . is lost, as though by some edict a fury had been let loose to commit every crime."[1] In an attempt to mitigate this brutality, Grotius synthesized elements from earlier naturalist and positivist juristic thought regarding those circumstances under which war might be initiated and how it should be waged upon its commencement. His pioneering *De jure belli ac pacis* ultimately provided the legal underpinnings for a period of relative stability in Europe lasting from the Peace of Westphalia until the French Revolution.[2]

However, the Napoleonic era had a deleterious affect on the legal order engendered by Grotius. In the aftermath of the Congress of Vienna, the question was raised whether or not it was ill-conceived to support laws which specified when war might be used as a method of national redress. As one writer put it,

In dealing with any other form of evil one's first impulse is to have the legislature or congress pass a law making the practice illegal and criminal. If that is the way to deal with ordinary grievances, why not try the beaten path with the greatest of all wrongs? We want not 'laws of war' but 'laws against war' as we have laws against murder and burglary.[3]

Yet other writers were not convinced that this was feasible. For them, international law was very much like the "annoying grandmother who, no longer able to tell her own children how to behave, insists on telling her children's children what to do."[4] Thus as they saw it, changes in legal output would not produce any noticeable impact.

Not surprisingly, the debate had a bearing upon how individuals viewed international arbitration. Champions of peaceful settlement procedures extolled the virtues of arbitration, while skeptics doubted its capacity to replace war as a mode of national redress.[5] Obviously, this debate raises a second issue for empirical research. It is not only important to understand the causes of international arbitration, but it is also important to know something about its consequences. Thus far the scope, amplitude, and intensity of arbitral activity have been treated as dependent variables, and various attributes of the international system have been used as independent variables to find what conditions have historically caused increases in arbitral activity. In order to determine the consequences of international arbitration, the scope, amplitude, and intensity of arbitral activity will now be treated as independent variables, and selected dimensions of central system war will become dependent variables.

Does Arbitration Beget Peace?

Any assessment of the consequences of a given activity must begin with some statement about the kinds of effects that will be examined. In its broadest sense, impact analysis includes both direct and indirect effects, as well as symbolic and tangible plus intended and unintended effects. The focus here will be on one direct, tangible, intended effect: the capacity of arbitration to reduce the amount of war in the international system.

Proposition 20.1: There is no relationship between arbitral activity and the onset of war.

Proposition 20.2: There is an inverse relationship between arbitral activity and the onset of war. According to Tucker, "It is naiveté, not sophistication, to believe that the convictions statesmen and nations profess and the justifications they urge in defense of their actions have no effect on the policies they pursue."[6] Rather than comprising a facade used to deceive others, these beliefs, he stresses, actually do influence behavior. This premise underlies much of the speculation about the ability of legal norms to reduce war. One school of thought argues that the convictions held by statesmen could be harnessed to prevent nations from utilizing force if the value of arbitration was promoted by various members of the global community. While this movement for the outlawry of war gained support from a broad spectrum of individuals, its program was not without critics.[7] But even many of its critics noted that while legal norms and institutions may not totally prevent the onset of war, they have limited its destructiveness. Corbett,[8] for example, sees an inverse relationship between growth in laws of war and the severity of interstate conflict. Similarly, Padelford and Lincoln conclude that "agreed norms and rules of conduct contained in the law . . . establish limits upon the exercise of sheer power . . . without which international relations would be anarchic."[9]

Yet several alternative interpretations of the relationship between force and the international legal culture also exist. On the one hand, it is asserted that norms are "qualifiers" of behavior which have not always been operative.[10] On the other hand we are told that contrary to Falk's view,[11] law functions principally as a tactical device,[12] and otherwise "has done not much more than apply a thin veneer of respectability to all kinds of behavior, some of it outrageous."[13] Finally it has been suggested that it is "too simple to believe that the way to achieve peace is to avoid war."[14] "To have peace, it is still necessary not only to prepare for war, but also on occasion to fight one; and to fight a war resolutely if one is to have a reasonably good and long peace."[15] In short, considerable disagreement may be found over the question of whether arbitration and other amicable settlement procedures really help preserve international peace, and this disagreement will not be resolved until measurement replaces metaphysics in the analysis of this question.

One of the most serious problems in measuring war is that there seems to be almost as many definitions of the concept as there are writers. The operational definition and historical data used here have been formulated by Singer and Small.[16] In order to be classified as an international war, a conflict must involve: at least one political entity with a population of 500,000 and/or diplomatic recognition by France or Great Britain; and over 1,000 battle casualties among all participants. As in the case of arbitration where we chose to analyze different dimensions of the phenomenon rather than use a simple frequency count for our dependent variable, so too shall we examine different dimensions of war. Specifically, two onset measures of central system war will be employed: (1) magnitude, or the number of nation-months resulting from all wars which began during the 1815-1965 time span; and (2) severity, or the number of battle-connected deaths resulting from all wars which began during the 1815-1965 time span. Armed with these two operational indicators of war, it is now possible to put forth the hypothesis that will be tested for the purpose of making an inference about propositions 20.1 and 20.2. Simply stated, it is expected that all three measures of arbitral activity will be inversely related to the magnitude and severity of war begun.

Table 5.1 gives the Pearson product-moment correlations between delta values of the scope, amplitude, and intensity of arbitral activity and delta values of the magnitude and severity of war begun, where the independent variables have been lagged one time unit. Since the analyses reported in Chapter 2 showed some notable changes in legal norms pertaining to arbitration and the use of force following 1914, three temporal periods were examined: pre-World War I, post-World War I, and the entire time span between 1815 and 1965. Although the hypothesized negative direction appeared in sixteen of the eighteen correlations listed in the table, most of these associations are not particularly strong. The strongest correlations occurred prior to World War I between the scope of arbitral activity and the magnitude and severity of war. Thus when a greater proportion of central system members used arbitration to settle their quarrels, the amount of central system war tended to decline. Interestingly enough, as pointed out in Chapter 2, the perceived salience of arbitration as a mode of conflict resolution covaried historically with the scope rather than the amplitude or intensity of arbitral activity.

Despite the moderate strength of the two relationships involving scope prior to 1914, the proportion of central system members using arbitration appears to have had little import after World War I. To some extent, the amplitude of arbitral activity became more consequential, but overall there does not seem to be any noteworthy linkage between an increase in the percentage of major powers participating in arbitral settlements at a given period in time and the amount of war which followed. By way of contrast, the correlations involving the intensity of arbitral activity remained fairly

Table 5.1   **Bivariate Correlations Between Arbitral Activity and the Onset of War**

| | Lagged Dimension of Arbitral Activity | | |
	Scope	Amplitude	Intensity
Amount of War Begun			
Magnitude			
Pre-World War I	−.62	.10	−.37
Post-World War I	−.12	−.23	−.33
Entire Span	−.26	−.09	−.30
Severity			
Pre-World War I	−.56	.01	−.24
Post-World War I	−.10	−.10	−.21
Entire Span	−.18	−.05	−.17

stable from one temporal domain to the next. But like the other two dimensions of arbitral activity, intensity has a greater impact on the magnitude of war than on its severity. Furthermore, like scope, intensity had a greater impact before World War I than after its outbreak. In sum, the directions of the bivariate relationships generally conform to what would be predicted by proposition 20.2, but the strength of these relationships makes it difficult to reject proposition 20.1 without probing the data further.

Besides looking at bivariate relationships, it should also prove helpful to examine the relative potency and additive impact of the three arbitration variables. Table 5.2 presents the results from a stepwise multiple regression analysis of the magnitude and severity of central system war begun. As can be seen by their entry in either the first (X_1) or second (X_2) step in each regression equation, scope (SCP) and intensity (INT) have the greatest impact upon war. In contrast, amplitude (AMP) only appears in half of the equations, and when it does, it stands as the least potent (X_3) of the three independent variables. Thus the percentage of states using arbitration and the importance of the issues they arbitrate bear far more on reducing war than the amount of arbitration which takes place among the major powers.

Table 5.2 Multivariate Correlations Between Arbitral Activity and the Onset of War

Amount of War Begun	Lagged Dimension of Arbitral Activity				
	R	R^2	X_1	X_2	X_3
Magnitude					
Pre-World War I	.69	.48	SCP	INT	—
Post-World War I	.39	.15	INT	SCP	—
Entire span	.40	.16	INT	SCP	AMP
Severity					
Pre-World War I	.60	.36	SCP	INT	AMP
Post-World War I	.27	.07	INT	SCP	AMP
Entire span	.25	.06	SCP	INT	—

Two other findings may be observed in the table. On the one hand, the multiple coefficients of determination show that the degree of arbitral activity had a greater impact on the onset of war prior to 1914 than it did afterwards. On the other hand, these statistics also indicate that we can better account for the size of ensuing wars than we can for their destructiveness. To put the matter another way, during its heyday, international arbitration appears to have exerted a dampening effect on the magnitude of war. Its impact on the severity of war was somewhat less, but nonetheless it was far greater than anything found in the aftermath of World War I.

Having thus portrayed the additive impact and relative contribution of the three independent variables upon each specific dependent variable, we may now focus our attention on the overall relation between the arbitration and the war variables taken as combined groups. Canonical correlation will be used to accomplish this research task. It derives a linear composite from both sets of variables through least squares analysis, and then finds the maximum correlation between the two sets. Because canonical correlation is a generalization of multiple regression with m dependent variables, more than one equation is calculated and more than one canonical correlation is produced. The trace correlation provides a measure of the relationship between all of the resulting canonical correlations. Therefore the square of the trace correlation gives the proportion of variance in one set of variables which can be accounted for by the other.[17] When a canonical correlation analysis was performed on the three arbitration variables and the two war variables for the entire time span under investigation, the squared trace correlation indicated that only 14 percent of the variance in central system war could be accounted for by arbitral activity. However, when the pre-World War I period was examined, the figure rose to 34 percent. Thus while a linear composite of the arbitration variables still could not explain much of the variance in a linear composite of the war variables, the results of the canonical correlation analysis nonetheless upheld the earlier finding that arbitration had its greatest impact in the century following the Congress of Vienna.

Some Final Caveats

Before going on to discuss the conclusions that may be drawn from these results, let us first issue a few warnings about the inferences that will be made. Ever since Plato's *Theaetetus*, philosophers have typically held that an individual (*I*) knows proposition (*p*) if: (1) *p* is true; (2) *I* believes that *p*; and (3) *I*'s epistemic justification *e* renders *p* evident for *I*. Recently questions raised by Edmund Gettier and others have led many philosophers to add a fourth condition; namely, that there is no counterevidence *q* such that *q* defeats *I*'s justifications.[18] Bearing this latter condition in mind, the individual who seeks to test propositions about international law must recognize that the greater the methodological limitations of his study, the more difficult it becomes to rule out counterevidence that might undermine the study's conclusions.

The results which have been presented thus far suffer from several limitations. First, because the magnitude and severity of those central system wars which actually occurred were regressed against arbitral activity, this study does not tell us what "potential" wars were prevented, or what might have happened without arbitration.

Second, the possibility of a nonrecursive relationship between the variables was not examined, except in the case of the three dimensions of arbitral activity. Nonetheless it is conceivable that reciprocal causation may exist among the other variables. On the one hand, preliminary evidence shows that there is a positive relationship between war termination and the incidence of arbitration. On the other hand, a close reading of the various works on system properties suggests that cultural and structural attributes are interdependent rather than independent. Hence future research on the impact of arbitration, as well as its systemic determinants, might be well advised to explore the applicability of feedback models.

Closely related to this potential limitation is a more basic concern over the design woven throughout the fabric of this study. In particular, it may be charged that the sequence of analysis performed from one chapter to the next does not guarantee that an empirical theory will ever be constructed. By entertaining only those variables which are put forth in the literature, some potent explanatory factors may be overlooked. Granted that the problem of excluded variables exists, there is nevertheless nothing to imply that this would be corrected by a different strategy. Moreover, since the field of international law is replete with theoretical propositions which very often come in antithetical pairs, it is extremely useful to be able to identify those which have some degree of empirical support. In saying this, it is taken as axiomatic that the process of falsification is central to scientific research and that the maxims, proverbs, and rules of thumb which comprise the conventional wisdom of the field are the most outstanding targets for its rigorous application.

Finally, the most general criticism that can be leveled against the results of this study is that it has merely produced an empirical pre-theory. No definitive theoretical explanation is advanced for either the causes or the consequences of international arbitration. Instead something else is given: an inductive-statistical account of which cultural and structural variables set the "climate" for arbitration, and the extent to which upswings in arbitration reduce the magnitude and severity of war. To be sure, this kind of explanation is indeterminate. But as Braithwaite insists, there is no completely final explanation in scientific research. At each stage of inquiry a "why" question can be asked about a generalization. While this question can be answered by incorporating that generalization into a more comprehensive set of generalizations, even these must be incorporated into a still higher level generalization if they themselves are to be explained.[19] But though there may be no ultimate end to this hierarchy of scientific explanation, a pre-theory based on evidence gathered through replicable procedures provides the kind of brush-clearing that allows one to sort out those variables which have minimal explanatory power from those which deserve further investigation to determine whether their observed relationships are genuine or spurious. Without this kind of beginning, the researcher becomes much like Alice who, when unable to tell the Cheshire Cat where she wanted to go, could not deny his advice that anywhere was as good as anywhere else.

Notes

1. Hugo Grotius, *The Law of War and Peace*, trans. L. R. Loomis (New York: Walter J. Black, 1949), pp. 10–11.

2. Despite intermittent hostilities (e.g., the War of the League of Augsburg, the Wars of Spanish and Austrian Succession, the Seven Years' War, etc.), many historians view this period as an interlude between the more ferocious Wars of Religion and Nationalism. Hoffmann characterizes the era as moderate partially because reciprocal laws of delimitation helped temper the scope of actor objectives and the means utilized to achieve them. This interpretation also underlies Guerlac's description of the waning influence of Machiavelli's *Arte della Guerra* and the concomitant growth of the laws of war. See Stanley Hoffmann, "International Systems and International Law," in *The International System: Theoretical Essays*, ed. Klaus Knorr and Sidney Verba (Princeton: Princeton University Press, 1961), pp. 215–17; Henry Guerlac, "Vauban: The Impact of Science on War," in *Makers of Modern Strategy, Military Thought from Machiavelli to Hitler*, ed. Edward Mead Earle (Princeton: Princeton University Press, 1943), p. 33. Also see Arnold J. Toynbee, *War and Civilization* (New York: Oxford University Press, 1950), p. 4.

3. S. Levinson as quoted in Frank M. Russell, *Theories of International Relations* (New York: Appleton-Century-Crofts, 1936), pp. 358–59.

4. J. Golden, "Force and International Law," in *The Use of Force in International Relations* (New York: Free Press, 1974), p. 196. Fried has summarized the reasoning behind this position in terms of four distinct theoretical critiques: (1) the "orphan" theory—international law is so idealistic that it is constantly disregarded; (2) the "harlot" theory—international law is so vague that it can be used to justify any foreign policy; (3) the "jailer" theory—international law is so defenseless that transgressors are not punished; and (4) the "never-never" theory—international law will remain unreliable until states agree to submit their conflicts to judicial settlement. John H. E. Fried, "International Law—Neither Orphan Nor Harlot, Neither Jailer Nor Never-Never Land," in *The Relevance of International Law*, ed. Karl Deutsch and Stanley Hoffmann (Garden City, N.Y.: Doubleday & Company, 1971), pp. 128-29.

5. Compare R. L. Jones, *International Arbitration as a Substitute for War Between Nations* (London: St. Andrew University, 1908); and Heinrich von Treitschke, "International Intercourse," in *The Theory of International Relations*, ed. M. G. Forsyth, H. M. A. Keens-Soper, and P. Savigeau (New York: Atherton Press, 1970), p. 339.

6. Robert W. Tucker, *The Just War, A Study in Contemporary American Doctrine* (Baltimore: Johns Hopkins University Press, 1960), p. 3.

7. See S. Levinson, "The Legal Status of War," *New Republic* 14 (March 1918): 171-73; and Walter Lippman, "The Outlawry of War," *Atlantic Monthly* 132 (August 1923): 245-53.

8. Percy E. Corbett, *Law in Diplomacy* (Princeton: Princeton University Press, 1959), p. 271.

9. Norman J. Padelford and George A. Lincoln, *the Dynamics of International Relations*, 2nd ed. (New York: Macmillan Co., 1967), p. 435.

10. Werner Levi, "The Relative Irrelevance of Moral Norms in International Politics," in *International Politics and Foreign Policy*, ed. James N. Rosenau, rev. ed. (New York: Free Press, 1969), p. 194; Quincy Wright, *A Study of War*, 2nd ed. (Chicago: University of Chicago Press, 1942), p. 893.

11. Richard A. Falk, *Legal Order in a Violent World* (Princeton: Princeton University Press, 1968), p. 74.

12. See Lawrence Scheinman, "The Berlin Blocade," in *International Law and the Political Crisis, An Analytic Casebook*, ed. Lawrence Scheinman (Boston: Little, Brown & Company, 1968), p. 39; or W. Friedmann and L. A. Collins, "The Suez Canal Crisis of 1956," Ibid., pp. 124-25.

13. George Modelski, *Principles of World Politics* (New York: Free Press, 1972), p. 337.

14. George Liska, *War and Order: Reflections on Vietnam and History* (Baltimore: Johns Hopkins University Press, 1968), p. 111.

15. Ibid.

16. J. David Singer and Melvin Small, *The Wages of War 1816-1965: A Statistical Handbook* (New York: John Wiley & Sons, 1972), Chaps. 2-3, 7.

17. For a more elaborate discussion, see J. W. Hooper, "Simultaneous

Equations and Canonical Correlation Theory," *Econometrica,* 27 (April 1959): 245–56.

18. Some of the most influential papers on this topic are collected in George S. Pappas and Marshall Swain, eds., *Essays on Knowledge and Justification* (Ithica: Cornell University Press, 1978).

19. R. B. Braithwaite, *Scientific Explanation* (London: Cambridge University Press, 1968), p. 347.

CHAPTER 6

Conclusion

With these caveats in mind, let us conclude with some observations about where we have gone thus far. This study constitutes a preliminary attempt to apply quantitative methods to the study of international arbitration. These methods were selected because they allow us to make generalizations which can be sustained by reproducible evidence. Although arbitration has been used in many different cultural settings throughout recorded history to resolve international disputes, students of international law have nonetheless failed to determine empirically what systemic conditions are associated with its use, and what impact it has had upon the onset of war. Indeed, one has only to skim the literature on arbitration to find support for Gray's claim that "on no subject of human interest, except theology, has there been so much loose writing and nebulous speculation as on international law."[1]

What is surprising is that the bulk of this literature claims to be part of a science of international law. Yet this turns out to be something quite different from what is commonly thought of as a science in the field of international relations. Science, as it has long been conceived of in legal research, implies "a systematic classification of the principles and rules of international law accompanied by an analysis of their origin and nature and their place in the general field of judicial relations."[2] Thus scientific analysis is equated with an investigation of the logical consistency between certain a priori standard of justice and those laws which made up the legal order in question. Even during periods when individuals sought to disloge their research from these transcendental first principles and looked instead for the source of legal norms in ongoing state behavior (e.g., Moser and Martins), or in the scholarly renditions (e.g., Bynkershoek) and official documentary records (e.g., Rachel) compiled on the historical conduct of diplomatic affairs, their results still remained impressionistic. That is, they were based on "a partial selection of relevant material" in which the criteria for selection were "arbitrary reflections of the researcher's values, national locus, and imperfect factual knowledge."[3] To put it very simply, what has more often than not passed for scientific research in international law has been atheoretical in design and transempirical in method.[4]

In contrast to this view of research, most scholars who engage in the quantitative study of international relations would agree with Runciman that the term science only becomes meaningful when "a particular area of human behaviour is isolated and a theory (or model) of a general 'if . . . then' form is put forward to explain it."[5] Throughout this study an attempt has been made to rework the assertions in the literature on international arbitration into theoretical propositions of an "if . . . then" form. Once this was done, they were transformed into testable hypotheses and subjected to empirical analysis. As a result of this methodological procedure, several contingency generalizations have been made about arbitral activity. Of course, these generalizations may be explained in different ways, just as the association between push and movement is explained in different ways by Aristotle, Galileo, and Newton. But until one first discovers what relationships exist in the empirical world, it is difficult to imagine how one will ever be able to invent a theory that can account for them.

The first set of relationships we have generalized about pertain to the scope of arbitral activity. Our data show that the percentage of central system members who used arbitration to resolve their disputes climbed from the 1830s through the 1890s, but fell off somewhat after the turn of the century. Although we cannot account for this pattern very well by looking at the attributes of the international system, changes in the perceived salience of arbitration do appear to have a noteworthy impact on the scope of arbitral activity. As arbitration became more widely accepted as an important mode of conflict resolution, an upswing occurred in the number of states which used arbitration. Furthermore, as the scope of arbitral activity increased, the magnitude and severity of war decreased.

The second set of relationships we have explored focused on temporal changes in the amplitude of arbitral activity. Throughout the century and a half following the Congress of Vienna, the proportion of major powers involved in arbitrations gradually declined. According to our analysis results, amplitude tended to decrease following previous decreases in the concentration of capabilities in the hands of a few major powers and increases in the movement of capability shares between powers. In other words, when there was a high degree of capability concentration and little movement, a larger proportion of major powers used arbitration. However, increases in amplitude have had very little impact on subsequent decreases in either the magnitude or severity of war.

The third set of relationships examined in this study centered on the intensity of arbitral activity. Of the three dimensions of arbitration we have analyzed, we can best account for changes in the importance of the issues which were arbitrated. As in the case of amplitude, the intensity of arbitral activity increased whenever there was a prior increase in capability concentration and a decrease in capability movement. Unlike amplitude, decreases in status inconsistency resulted in upswings in intensity, and these upswings had a moderately negative impact on both the magnitude and severity of war.

Overall, there appear to be two general areas of convergence between these conclusions and the findings from other system-level studies of international war. The first area of convergence deals with the effect of changes in capability distribution over time. We have noted that a high stable concentration of capabilities among a small number of major powers has been directly related to upward turns in the level of arbitral activity. Moreover, increases in the scope and intensity of arbitration resulted in decreases in the magnitude of war begun. Therefore we suspect that changes in both the level of capability concentration and the rate of capability movement act directly to decrease the amount of interstate war by reducing the amount of uncertainty throughout the global community, while at the same time acting to decrease the probability of war indirectly by providing an environment conducive to conflict resolution through third-party arbitration. Although more research is needed in order to ascertain whether this deduction corresponds with actual behavior, initial tests have shown "the preponderance and stability school's predictions to be closer to historical reality than those of the parity and fluidity school."[6]

A second important area of convergence between this study and other quantitative examinations of the impact of system attributes upon war can be seen in the findings which emerged from our analysis of the concept of status hierarchy. Our research indicated that the intensity of arbitral activity increased when the international system moved toward a stable hierarchy of rank positions. That is, during periods marked by high levels of status inconsistency and status mobility states tended to arbitrate questions in low salience issue-areas rather than those which dealt with the conduct of hostilities. Since the intensity of arbitral activity has been inversely related to the magnitude of war begun, we would expect status hierarchy to influence conflict behavior both directly and also indirectly by decreasing the intensity of arbitral activity within the international system.[7] Again, additional research is needed to determine whether this deduction fits with historical reality, but preliminary tests suggest that "status inconsistency and war are linked by not one, but several sequences."[8]

To sum up, international legal studies have historically devoted more attention to developing law-in-books than describing law-in-action. However, during the past half century interest in the relationship between international law and politics has grown. Throughout the 1930s and 40s, for instance, scholars focused their energies first on an attempt to outlaw war and second on how to set up an international organization that would preserve peace. But by the 1950s, many legal scholars had jettisoned their concern with these kinds of broad issues and concentrated instead upon the concrete daily problems of transnational industry, finance, and agriculture.[9] For those who retained their interest in the issues of war and peace, the 1960s were a time when analytical frameworks were borrowed from other disciplines in the belief that new ways of conceptualizing the nexus between international law and politics would some-how advance international legal research. Frameworks taken from decision-making, structural-functional, and general systems approaches were thus said to have heuristic value. Still, as Stephens has argued, to be heuristic is not in itself to be scientific:

Newton found it of heuristic value to sit under an apple tree, but we can hardly expect such an endeavor will be beneficial for students of politics. Nor can we assume that what has been a heuristic value for others will be so for us. We have already had enough heuristic formulations to last most students of politics a lifetime, and it is now time to ask for results.[10]

But results are contingent upon theory and, as Torgerson has put it, "the development of a theoretical science . . . would seem virtually impossible unless its variables can be measured adequately."[11]

Measurement, then, is the sine qua non of science. The measurements and data analyses undertaken in this study have been organized according to a wide inductivist conception of scientific inquiry. They began with a univariate graphic analysis of a set of first-order propositions about diachronic fluctuations in arbitral activity and certain legal norms which were thought to influence the scope, amplitude, and intensity of arbitration. Next a group of second-order propositions pertaining to the association between various systemic attributes and arbitral activity were investigated via bivariate correlational analysis. The relative potencies of those variables which survived the bivariate tests were then determined by means of a stepwise multiple regression analysis. Finally, the impact of arbitration upon the magnitude and severity of war was examined through correlation and regression analysis.

The major conclusion which emerged from this study was that the use of international arbitration to resolve highly salient issues occurred most often when the following conditions were present in the international environment: (1) a preponderance of capabilities were concentrated in the hands of a few major powers; (2) little movement of capabilities took place between these powers; and (3) a consistent and stable rank order of states existed below the major powers. When these conditions occurred, arbitration was generally considered to be an important mode of conflict resolution by the international legal culture. When they broke down, the perceived importance of arbitration decreased, less states used arbitration to settle their differences, and the magnitude and severity of war increased.

Of course, it may be argued that conclusions such as these are not particularly useful since system-level theories lack policy relevance. This line of reasoning overlooks the fact that many of the decisions made by statesmen are based on how these individuals think about the causal connections between macro phenomena. If system-level research can falsify some of the inviting but erroneous elements within their conventional wisdom, then a significant contribution will have been made.

At the onset of this study, it was argued that one way to make this contribution would be to recast traditional speculations into propositional form and confront these propositions with reproducible evidence. Once this kind of reconnaissance work has been done, it then becomes possible to put together an empirically-grounded pre-theory out of those propositions which have been supported by the evidence. To borrow a metaphor from Waltz, impressionistic studies of international law may produce insights, but they remain like a number of pearls and glass beads lying around loose. The value of the pearls may be great, but to separate them from the beads a jeweller's glass is required, and, once the pearls have been selected, their value can only be enhanced by placing them together in a setting or on a string.[12] At the least, it is hoped that the present study has demonstrated that social scientific methodology can serve as a jeweller's glass which, when applied to the analysis of legal phenomena such as arbitration, can help us sort out those intuitively plausible but erroneous assertions that abound in the literature on international law.

Notes

1. John Chipman Gray, *Nature and Sources of the Law* (New York: Macmillan Co., 1927), p. 127.

2. Charles Fenwick, *International Law* (New York: Appleton-Century-Crofts, 1965), p. 53.

3. Richard A. Falk, "New Approaches to the Study of International Law," in *New Approaches to International Relations*, ed. Morton A. Kaplan (New York: St. Martin's Press, 1968), p. 369.

4. Sheikh goes one step further. In his estimation the basic writers on international law share a "fundamental opposition to the viewpoint of the social sciences." Similarly, Falk points out that most contemporary international lawyers profess to be against social scientific theory. See Ahmed Sheikh, *International Law and National Behavior* (New York: John Wiley & Sons, 1974), p. 8; and Richard A. Falk, *The Status of Law in International Society* (Princeton: Princeton University Press, 1970), p. 8.

5. W. G. Runciman, *Social Science and Political Theory*, 2nd ed. (Cambridge: Cambridge University Press, 1971), p. 5.

6. J. David Singer, Stuart Bremer, and John Stuckey, "Capability Distribution, Uncertainty, and Major Power War, 1820-1965," in *Peace, War, and Numbers*, ed. by Bruce M. Russett (Beverly Hills, Calif.: Sage Publications, 1972), p. 46.

7. Michael D. Wallace, *War and Rank Among Nations* (Lexington, Mass.: D. C. Heath and Company, 1973), p. 108.

8. Ibid.

9. See Irvin White, "International Law," in *International Systems: A Behavioral Approach*, ed. Michael Haas (New York: Chandler Publishing

Co., 1974), pp. 257–58; and Kenneth W. Thompson, "The Origins, Uses and Problems of Theory in International Relations," in *The Role of Theory in International Relations*, ed. Horace V. Harrison (Princeton: D. Van Nostrand Company, 1964), p. 52.

10. Jerone Stephens, "An Appraisal of Some System Approaches in the Study of International Systems," *International Studies Quarterly* 16 (September 1972): 348.

11. W. S. Torgerson, *Theory and Methods of Scaling* (New York: John Wiley & Sons, 1958), p. 2.

12. Kenneth N. Waltz, "Political Philosophy and the Study of International Relations," in *Theoretical Aspects of International Relations*, ed. William T. R. Fox (Notre Dame: University of Notre Dame Press, 1959), p. 66.

Index

About the Author

Dr. Raymond is a member of the Department of Political Science at Boise State University, Boise, Idaho. He was the co-director of the Conference on Military Policy Evaluation at the Strategic Studies Institute, U.S. Army War College, in 1977, and of the Southeast Regional Conference on National Security Affairs in 1974. His articles have appeared widely in journals of international studies; he is co-editor of *International Events and the Comparative Analysis of Foreign Policy* and *Military Policy Evaluation: Quantitative Applications*, and is the co-author of *Comparative European Politics: The Other Western Europe*.

About the Author